Praise for *How to End Injustice Everywhere*

"Dr. Joy leverages her deep training and ethos towards promoting diversity and culture, as well as respect both for humans and non-humans alike. She delves into questions that gaze at us straight in the eyes, like pink elephants in the room, that the world through willful ignorance or otherwise has had the inability to see. Until now. *How to End Injustice Everywhere* sheds light on how the relational will always triumph, and how through understanding the drivers and levers of injustice, a just world may be closer than we dare to dream."—**HRH Dr. Anjhula Mya Singh Bais**, Chair, International Board, Amnesty International

"In *How to End Injustice Everywhere*, Melanie Joy powerfully explains how our attempts to end injustice must be inclusive, because the psychology that informs all forms of injustice—against humans, animals, and the environment—is the same."
—**Max H. Bazerman**, Straus Professor, Harvard Business School and author of *Better, Not Perfect* and *Complicit*

"*How to End Injustice Everywhere* is a thought-provoking book that sheds light on the way we think about oppression and social justice."
—**Marianne Williamson**, speaker, activist, author of four #1 *New York Times* bestselling books, and US presidential candidate

HOW TO
END
INJUSTICE
EVERYWHERE

**understanding the common denominator
driving all injustices, to create a better
world for humans, animals, and the planet**

MELANIE JOY, PhD

Lantern Publishing & Media ● Woodstock and Brooklyn, NY

2023
Lantern Publishing & Media
PO Box 1350
Woodstock, NY 12498
www.lanternpm.org

Printed in the United States of America

Library of Congress Cataloging-in-Publication Data

Names: Joy, Melanie, author.
Title: How to end injustice everywhere : understanding the common denominator driving all injustices to create a better world for humans, animals, and the planet / Melanie Joy, PhD.
Description: Woodstock, NY : Lantern Publishing & Media, 2023. | Includes bibliographical references.
Identifiers: LCCN 2023001817 (print) | LCCN 2023001818 (ebook) | ISBN 9781590566862 (paperback) | ISBN 9781590566879 (epub)
Subjects: LCSH: Social justice. | Justice—Psychological aspects. | Human ecology. | Human-animal relationships. | Interpersonal relations—Psychological aspects.
Classification: LCC HM671 .J69 2023 (print) | LCC HM671 (ebook) | DDC 303.3/72—dc23/eng/20230124
LC record available at https://lccn.loc.gov/2023001817
LC ebook record available at https://lccn.loc.gov/2023001818

For each of you who is helping to create a more relational world, whether you're working quietly in the background or marching on the front lines. Thank you.

TABLE OF CONTENTS

About the Author
About the Publisher

ACKNOWLEDGEMENTS

I AM DEEPLY GRATEFUL FOR the support of the many people who made writing this book possible. I thank my Beyond Carnism team of compassionate and hardworking change agents for holding down the fort and providing me with much-needed assistance. I'm so grateful to Adrian Ramsay for his invaluable listening and insights, and a very special thanks goes to Dawn Moncrief, who has been an unending source of strength, inspiration, and wisdom. I am grateful to my agent, Marilyn Allen, who helped me shift the trajectory of the original book, and to the folks at Berrett-Koehler, who graciously enabled me to reclaim rights to it in order to create this one. I am especially grateful to my editor, Anna Leinberger, who went above and beyond to birth this new project—and to my other wonderful editors, Lucy Anne Evans and Jo and Dianne Hildebrand. I thank Krista Hiddema for her insights, and I thank Martin Rowe for guiding me toward Lantern and Brian Normoyle for providing me with a home for the book, and for all his understanding and support. I also thank the many people whose insights and feedback helped me hone my ideas when I was originally developing them for the earlier version of this book: Jens Tuider, Aryenish Birdie, Carolyn Zaikowski, Liz Ross, Melanie

Gold, Chantal Prinsloo, Victoria Yates, Wilke Seekles, Elliot Gold, Bonnie Gramlich, Vique Mora, Alexandra Navarro, Silvania Pezzetta, Beatrice Frasl, Julia Aumüller, Diane Coetzer, Orit Kamir, Paul Gorski, Leah Edgerton, and especially Gero Schomaker. As always, I am tremendously grateful to the amazing people whose financial support is the reason my team and I can do the work we do: a massive thank-you to Jim Greenbaum and Meghan O'Brien Lowery; Verónica Diaz Carrai and Darren Sparks; Ari Nessel, Birju Pandya, and Alan Darer; Kathy Head; Owen Gunden, Sabina Makhdomi, Rockwell Schwartz, and John Boland; and Chuck and Jennifer Laue and Tom Conger; a huge thanks to Walter Abrego and his colleagues for making it possible for a vitally important campaign to be created around the concepts in this book; and another huge thanks to our supporters who prefer to remain unnamed. I am grateful to the wonderful Miriam Schafaczek for all her behind-the-scenes work and support that have kept me intact in so many ways, and to Wolfgang Hußmann for the added positivity and encouragement he's brought to me. I am beyond grateful to my very dear friends Susan Solomon, Kathy Freston, Ria Rehberg, and Robin Flynn-Joven, for keeping me psychologically and emotionally nourished and for providing more support than they know, and to Eric Robinson for helping me recharge and stay inspired. And as with all my work, I am so grateful to Sebastian Joy, my husband, muse, and partner in working to cultivate a more relational world.

PREFACE

I WROTE THIS BOOK WITH one goal in mind: to provide the people who are working to create a better world with information and tools to support their efforts. I have tremendous respect and gratitude for those who care about our planet and its human and nonhuman inhabitants, and who are committed to helping end the extensive and intensive suffering and harm caused by widespread injustice. You are the reason I hold on to hope.

This book is not meant to be a primer on ending injustice, nor is it meant to oversimplify what is clearly a complex problem. There are many excellent books and other tools covering a wide array of issues related to the subject that examine injustice from multiple perspectives. This book is meant to be a complement to other works, providing what I hope will be additional insights and tools.[1] It's also not meant to explain what kinds of strategies, tactics, campaigns, or other types of actions are appropriate to help end injustice. There are plenty of great materials on those topics, which have been produced by highly experienced advocates and organizers.

I wrote this book because I believe that a missing link in the existing literature on progressive social change is an understanding of the psychological—most notably, the relational—drivers of injustice. And I believe that illuminating these drivers, and how they are expressed through our interactions and relationships, can help hasten our efforts to create a more just world. In other words, I am suggesting *not* that injustice isn't a deeply entrenched, institutionalized reality that is maintained by powerful social structures, but rather that examining these structures through a relational lens can help deepen our understanding of unjust dynamics and support our efforts to change them.

Understanding the relational underpinnings of injustice helps us target the problem at its roots, rather than address only one or a few of its countless manifestations. This doesn't mean that we take on multiple causes at once, but that we understand that the mentality (and its resultant behaviors) that drives all forms of injustice is the same. We take an *inclusive* approach to ending injustice. This means that we take into account the interests of not only human beings, but also of nonhuman beings. Moral philosophers have long argued that *speciesism*—the ideology that places animals on a hierarchy of moral worth, with humans at the top—reflects human supremacy, an attitude that, when examined, proves to be like other forms of supremacy and is similarly morally indefensible.[2] Most people are not aware of the philosophical case for including nonhuman animals in conversations about justice, and those who are aware of it often don't act on it, as philosophical arguments can easily remain abstractions, lofty ideals at best. Moreover, movements for justice for nonhuman animals are generally not labeled as such: the animal rights movement aims to secure basic rights for nonhuman animals, and the vegan movement aims to end animal[3] exploitation. These movements obviously overlap and could be considered submovements of a broader animal justice movement. (For the sake of clarity and simplicity, I've focused on the vegan movement in this book, but all points apply to the animal justice movement more broadly.) For these reasons, many progressive people who support movements for social and environmental justice view the animal justice movement as fundamentally different from—or even in opposition to—these other movements. Looking at injustice through a relational lens, though, can help us understand why we'll never end up with a truly just and compassionate world if we work to end injustice against human beings while disregarding injustice against nonhuman beings.[4]

I use examples throughout the book to help clarify the concepts presented, and I've tried to make these examples as diverse as possible. Many examples, however, reflect those forms of injustice that I expect most readers will be familiar with, such as white privilege, male privilege, and class privilege. I chose to use such examples so that readers could more easily relate to and understand the material, and I don't mean to minimize other forms of privilege.

The concepts in *How to End Injustice Everywhere* have been informed by the work of countless scholars and advocates, work that has been invaluable in illuminating paths to understanding injustice through the fog that obscures it.[5] These concepts were first published in my book *Powerarchy* in 2019. Since the publication of *Powerarchy*, however, my thinking around the subject evolved, and I felt that it was important to update that book in order to accommodate my newer ideas and modified framework. Because the changes I ended up making were relatively comprehensive, I decided to take *Powerarchy* out of print and republish the text as a new book, the book you are reading now.

How to End Injustice Everywhere is for anyone who is doing the vitally important work of ending injustice. This work is urgent, and I am humbled and inspired by the dedication, compassion, and brilliance of the many people who are helping create a better world for us all. I hope this book will make a contribution to those efforts.

PART 1

UNDERSTANDING INJUSTICE

Nonrelational Systems and Dynamics

Injustice anywhere is a threat to justice everywhere.
—Martin Luther King, Jr.

1
FORMULA FOR A BETTER WORLD

*Teaching a child not to step on a caterpillar is [almost] as
valuable to the child as it is to the caterpillar.*
—Bradley Miller

WHEN I WAS FOUR YEARS old, I killed someone. And forty-three
years later, I received the Ahimsa Award for my work on global
nonviolence.

Of course, on that fateful day in 1970, I had no idea that
my actions would set me on a journey of discovery that would
transform the way I understood and related to myself and the
world, and that would lead me to write award-winning books and
establish an international NGO to help others experience similar
transformation.

It was a hot summer day, and I was with my parents on my
father's fishing boat, my favorite place in the world to be. And then
I caught my first fish. My parents clapped and laughed and told
me how proud they were, but I felt confused and distraught. As I
watched the fish I'd pulled out of the ocean flop on the floor of the
boat gasping for oxygen, all I could feel was sadness. And guilt.

After that day, my father's boat, which had once been a source of joy, became a trigger for distress. And seafood, which I had loved, sickened me to the point where I could no longer eat it without vomiting.

My emotions and body were reacting to a paradox that my young brain wasn't developed enough to understand. I couldn't reconcile how caring people—my own parents at that—could harm others and neither see nor feel troubled by this contradiction. My parents had instilled in me a strong commitment to practicing the Golden Rule—to treating others the way I'd want to be treated if I were in their position. So had my teachers, the ministers at our church, and nearly every other adult who influenced my development. Yet it seemed that everywhere I turned, this supposedly highest principle was being violated, and nobody was the least bit concerned.

Whether it was my father killing fish for enjoyment, movies depicting men subduing emotionally distraught women by slapping them across the face (it was the 1970s, after all), or children bullying each other on the playground in plain sight of unconcerned teachers, the relational paradox I was witnessing was the same. The Golden Rule, a principle meant to guide the way we relate to others, was as disregarded as it was esteemed—and this contradiction was utterly invisible.

It wasn't until more than two decades later that I was finally able to comprehend and articulate this relational paradox, a phenomenon I'd been increasingly sensitized to over the years. I had become deeply concerned with social injustices, and I found myself confounded by the dysfunctional state of humanity that not only allowed for but perpetrated widespread suffering and harm. What, I wondered, makes people turn away from—rather than challenge—atrocities? Why do some of the same people who stand on the streets demonstrating for human rights mistreat members of their own families? Why do those who claim to want a society based on compassion and fairness nevertheless vote and act against these values?

The answers to these questions came to me after another incident involving an animal, this time in the form of a hamburger. I was twenty-three years old, and I'd recently eaten a beef patty that was contaminated with campylobacter, the "salmonella" of the red-meat world. I wound up hospitalized and on intravenous antibiotics, and after that experience I found myself too disgusted to eat meat again. I became a vegetarian, sort of by accident.

In the process of learning about my new diet, I stumbled upon information about animal agriculture. What I learned shocked and horrified me. The extent of the needless suffering endured by billions of nonhuman animals and the environmental devastation caused by the industry were almost incomprehensible. But what disturbed me perhaps even more was that nobody I talked to about what I'd learned was willing to hear what I had to say. People's responses were nearly always along the lines of, "Don't tell me that—you'll ruin my meal," or to call me a radical vegan hippie propagandist (upon learning about the horrors of the dairy and egg industries, I'd stopped consuming all animal products). And these were my friends and family—conscientious, rational people who were committed to helping create a more just world and who genuinely cared about animals.

The Psychology of Violence and Nonviolence

Wanting to understand what it was that caused people to harbor these contradictory attitudes and behaviors—what enabled the relational paradox I first observed when I killed the fish—I enrolled in a doctoral program in psychology, where I studied the psychology of violence and nonviolence. What, I asked, enables caring people to participate in—or otherwise support—practices that harm others, be they human or nonhuman beings? And what, then, could help change such behaviors?

I narrowed the focus of my research to examine a specific expression of the relational paradox: the psychosociology of eating animals. I sought to understand how people who care about the wellbeing of animals nevertheless consume or otherwise kill them. I conducted interviews and surveys, and coded and analyzed responses. And what I discovered was that eating certain animals results from extensive social and psychological conditioning. This conditioning is the product of what I came to call *carnism*: the invisible belief system, or ideology, that conditions people to eat certain animals. Carnism causes naturally rational and empathic people to have distorted perceptions and to disconnect from their empathy so that they act against their values of justice and compassion without fully realizing what they're doing. In other words, carnism teaches us to violate the Golden Rule without knowing or caring that we're doing so.

My research led me not only to the discovery of carnism, but also to an understanding of how all violent or oppressive ideologies are structured. I had deconstructed the carnistic system, identifying and articulating the specific social and psychological defense mechanisms that keep it intact. And I came to realize that these same mechanisms exist in all oppressive systems. In other words, the same psychological (and social) mechanisms that enable us to harm nonhumans enable us to harm humans.

My theory of carnism became popularized through my book *Why We Love Dogs, Eat Pigs, and Wear Cows*. My hope was that the book would not only invite nonvegans to reflect on their relationship with farmed animals but also encourage all people, including vegans, to recognize how various oppressive systems influence the way they relate to others. To some extent, my hope was fulfilled: a number of people shared with me that they found the book applicable across issues and that they had become more conscientious about myriad forms of oppression.

If It's Not One "Ism," It's Another

But humans have a remarkable ability to compartmentalize, and vegans are no exception. Just as my attempts to raise awareness of carnism were met with resistance from my socially progressive, meat-eating family and friends, I found that my attempts to raise awareness of patriarchy, racism, and other oppressions not involving nonhuman animals caused some vegans to react defensively. I'd point out that although women made up about 80 percent of the vegan movement, the majority of its leaders were men. I'd also note that vegan outreach didn't always reflect the experiences and needs of BIPOC (Black, Indigenous, and People of Color)—something BIPOC vegans had been saying for some time.[1] My comments were largely disregarded and sometimes blatantly challenged—by people who admittedly had little to no literacy or awareness around the issues I was raising.

My experiences talking about social justice with a number of vegan advocates paralleled my experiences talking about veganism with a number of social justice advocates. It became clear to me that more often than not, people would step outside of one problematic "ism" only to land (or rather, remain) in others, while believing they'd somehow extricated themselves from all such "isms."

And this same phenomenon occurs across all relational dimensions. There are three primary dimensions in which people relate: the collective, or societal, dimension (how social groups relate), the interpersonal dimension (how two or several individuals relate), and the intrapersonal dimension (how one relates to oneself). People tend to assume that awareness and transformation in one dimension automatically lead to awareness and transformation in all three dimensions. Yet, people often step out of oppressive or abusive[2] (unjust) dynamics, or interactions, in one dimension only to stay stuck in such dynamics in one or both of the others. For example, people who are actively working toward more just social policies may nevertheless be verbally abusive to those they disagree with, engaging in the same kinds of behaviors in the interpersonal dimension that they're challenging in the societal one.[3]

The Common Denominator

My research led me to recognize that there is a fundamental commonality driving all forms of injustice, all forms of oppression and abuse. (Injustice—which is, by definition, unfairness, or unfair treatment—is manifested most commonly and problematically through oppression, and to a lesser extent through abuse.) When we look at various expressions of injustice in our world, and also in our personal lives, such as war, poverty, racism, patriarchy, animal exploitation, climate change, and domestic abuse, we can see that they all share a common denominator, which is relational dysfunction, or dysfunctional ways of relating—between social groups to other individuals, to other animals and the environment, and even to ourselves (we're always relating to ourselves through, for example, the choices we make that impact our future self and through our "self-talk," or internal dialogue). What this means is that a common denominator in ending these injustices, in transforming all these problems, is the opposite: relational function, or healthy ways of relating.[4]

Formula for a Better World

Healthy relating is based on a simple formula.[5] This formula applies to all three relational dimensions—the collective/

societal,[6] interpersonal, and intrapersonal—and to all kinds of relationships. It also applies to how we relate to other animals[7] and the environment. The formula applies equally to brief interactions and to long-term relationships; a relationship is, after all, a series of interactions. And, of course, it applies to how we communicate, since communication is the primary way we relate.

In a healthy relationship or interaction, we practice integrity and honor dignity. This leads to a sense of security and connection.

Formula for Healthy Relating

$$\frac{\text{practice integrity + honor dignity}}{\text{connection and security}}$$

Integrity is the alignment of our core moral values of compassion and justice[8] and our behaviors. We practice integrity when we act according to these values. Put simply, when we practice integrity, we treat others the way we would want to be treated if we were in their position; we treat them with respect.

Dignity is our sense of inherent worth. When we honor someone's dignity, we perceive and treat them as no less worthy of being treated with respect than anyone else.

And healthy relating, like most things in life, is not an either-or phenomenon. It exists on a spectrum. Rarely is an interaction or relationship fully healthy or dysfunctional. Rather, it's more or less so. On the healthy side of the spectrum are *relational* attitudes and behaviors. On the dysfunctional side are *nonrelational* attitudes and behaviors. Nonrelational attitudes and behaviors violate integrity, harm dignity, and lead to a sense of disconnection and insecurity.

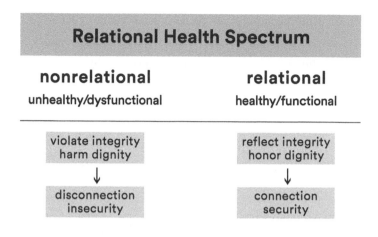

Consider your own experience. Think of a relationship in your life that you consider healthy. Chances are you trust that the other person will treat you with respect and you feel that they see you as no less worthy of being treated in such a way than anyone else. So you probably feel secure and connected with them. Now think of a relationship in your life that's not healthy—maybe it's with someone you haven't even met in person, such as an online troll. Chances are you don't feel that they treat you with respect or think of you as worthy of being treated so, and you feel insecure with and disconnected from them.

The Nonrelational Mentality

At the core of all relationally dysfunctional behaviors lies a specific mentality. This mentality is nonrelational: it causes us to think and therefore to feel and act in ways that run counter to the formula for healthy relating and that tend to ultimately bring about outcomes that are the opposite of what we want.

The nonrelational mentality is based on the belief in a *hierarchy of moral worth*: the belief that some individuals or groups are more worthy of moral consideration, of being treated with respect, than others. Believing in a hierarchy of moral worth essentially makes us feel justified in disrespecting and harming others (or ourselves, when we demean ourselves).

This belief in a hierarchy of moral worth can manifest—we can buy into and act upon it—in countless ways. Perhaps patriarchy has conditioned us to think of men and boys as more deserving of respect than women and girls and people of other genders. Perhaps carnism has conditioned us to believe that dogs are more deserving of being treated with kindness than pigs or chickens. Or perhaps we simply think we're more deserving of respect than those whose opinions or behaviors we disagree with.

Healthy and Dysfunctional Systems

It's not only our attitudes and behaviors that can be more or less healthy, or relational. So, too, can the systems to which we belong.

A system is a whole that's made up of two or more parts, or individuals. For example, your intimate partnership, family, and workplace are all systems, as are broader social arrangements such as capitalism, Catholicism, and racism. We even have an internal system, as we're always interacting with ourselves in various ways. For instance, you may have noticed that you have a voice in your head that's always talking to you.

On the nonrelational end of the relational health spectrum, the systems are oppressive and abusive. These *nonrelational systems** are those such as racism, patriarchy, carnism, a dysfunctional workplace, or an abusive interpersonal relationship.

The nonrelational mentality that lies at the core of and drives relational dysfunction is transmitted to us largely by the

---

* In this book, when I use the term "nonrelational systems," I am referring to both oppressive and abusive systems.

various nonrelational systems of which we're a part. And we take actions that reproduce this mentality without realizing that we're doing so. The nonrelational mentality compels us to indirectly support, or directly engage in, a range of harmful behaviors, from those that undermine the sense of security and connection in our interpersonal relationships to those that enable global atrocities. We may, for example, be proponents of social justice but nevertheless perceive people who are in prison for having committed violent crimes as morally inferior, as less worthy of our respect than others and their interests less deserving of consideration than others'.

Although nonrelational systems harm everyone who's a part of the systems, some individuals are more negatively impacted than others. Nonrelational systems create unjust power imbalances among the individuals within them, imbalances that increase over time. Consider, for example, the difference in power between two partners, one of whom is abusive and the other abused, or between social groups such as cisgender individuals and gender-nonconforming people. Those on the lower end of a power differential—and who are perceived as being on a lower rung of the hierarchy of moral worth—are harmed in far more ways and much more substantially than are those on the higher end.

Nonrelational systems cause us to violate the first precept of relating: the Golden Rule. And in so doing, they lie at the heart of the relational paradox.

Relational systems, by contrast, reflect and reinforce the Golden Rule. Relational systems are based on the recognition of the inherent dignity of all beings. Rather than creating insecurity, disconnection, and unjust power imbalances, they cultivate security and connection and lead to a balance of power.[9]

Relational Literacy

The fish I killed was the first of two individuals who shaped the trajectory of my life's work. The second was my dog, Fritz, whom I grew up with. The fish was my first relational casualty, and Fritz was my first friend. The fish taught me what it felt like to perpetrate relational dysfunction, and Fritz taught me what it felt like to cultivate relational health.

My relationships with these two animals led me to recognize both a *metaproblem* facing our world—relational dysfunction— and a *metasolution* to this problem—relational literacy. *Relational literacy* is the understanding of and ability to practice healthy ways of relating. Obviously, relational literacy isn't the only solution to all our problems, but it's foundational to all other solutions.

Despite the importance of relational literacy, most of us don't recognize its value, nor are we taught how to build it. It's striking that most of us have to learn complicated geometry that we'll probably never need to use, and yet we don't get a single formal lesson in how to relate in ways that are healthy—especially given that widespread injustice, the driver of the most serious problems facing our world, is not caused by the fact that people can't do geometry. We'll be unlikely to end injustice if we don't practice and promote healthy ways of relating.

How, for example, can we hope to have just governments and policies when so much of the populace not only tolerates but celebrates nonrelational attitudes and behaviors, such as toxic communication and political grandstanding and aggression? Surely, if our collective level of relational literacy weren't so low—if we weren't still living in the relational dark ages—we wouldn't elect relationally dysfunctional leaders or vote for relationally harmful policies.

And how can we hope to challenge widespread injustice if our very movements for justice reflect and drive the same nonrelational attitudes and behaviors we're working to transform? Indeed, when justice movements are more relational, their proponents—advocates—are more likely to exchange ideas openly and to learn and grow. The movements are better able to attract supporters, in large part because advocates are less likely to espouse the nonrelational, toxic communication that often involves shaming those who disagree with their views. Advocates are also less likely to burn out from the frustration, exhaustion, relationship breakdowns, self-neglect, and, often, traumatization common among people confronting injustices. And the more advocates build relational literacy, the less likely they are to fuel the epidemic infighting that can cause a movement to cannibalize itself.

The Metamission

I believe that a key obstacle to bringing about justice for all beings and the planet is the lack of a comprehensive, relational framework, or model, with which to understand injustice. I believe that the common tendency to view oppressive and abusive systems reductively—as more distinct from one another than they are, and as disconnected across the three relational dimensions (collective, interpersonal, and intrapersonal)—is in large part due to the fact that we have not fully identified the relational common denominator that underlies all forms of injustice.

If we hope to end all injustice, we need nothing short of a foundational shift in how we think about this issue. Until we make this shift, any attempt to bring about a more just, compassionate world will likely be an exercise in futility. It's not enough to address only *who* is oppressing or abusing *whom*. We need to understand the psychology underlying *how and why* we oppress and abuse in the first place. Otherwise, our efforts can lead us to trade one form of injustice for another. If we hope to end injustice, we need to change the way we relate.

When we recognize that all injustices share a nonrelational common denominator, we can better target the roots of injustice, and our movements for justice can become more unified and impactful. We can appreciate that whatever our specific mission (to achieve justice for humans, nonhuman animals, or the environment), our ultimate, collective mission—our shared *metamission*—is to create a more relational world.

2
OPPRESSION:
THE PROLIFERATION OF INJUSTICE

*If we don't get to the root of oppressive behavior, then we
risk reproducing the oppressive framework in our own
liberation movements.*
—Syl Ko

OPPRESSION IS THE UNJUST ALLOCATION and use of power. And
it's arguably the most notable driver and manifestation of injustice,
as well as the single greatest cause of human and nonhuman suffering
and of some of the most perilous environmental problems our planet
has ever known.* The countless manifestations of oppression range
from the seemingly benign to the catastrophic, from the micro (how
we treat individuals) to the macro (how we operate as a collective).
Rape, war, genocide, child abuse, poverty, climate change, factory
farming, terrorism, racism, casteism,[1] patriarchy—oppression is
manifested in any behavior or system that mirrors and supports the
unjust exercising of power and control over another or others.[2] And

---

* There is, of course, also significant suffering that is inherent in nature and not caused by
humans, experienced by wild animal populations, for example.

oppressive behaviors, as well as the attitudes that accompany them, are self-reinforcing: oppression begets oppression, in a feedback loop. So ending oppression—intercepting and transforming the deeply ingrained patterns of thinking and behaving that form the foundation of global suffering and destruction—is arguably the single most important undertaking of our time, as well as a key to ending injustice.

There have been countless efforts to end various forms of oppression over the course of human history, and with increasing awareness of social problems and structural inequalities, more and more oppressions are, fortunately, being dismantled. Despite such changes, however, history manages to repeat itself. Often, when one oppression is diminished, a new one emerges or an existing one is bolstered. For example, at the same time that policies are constructed to limit anti-Semitic practices,[3] anti-Muslim legislation is put into effect;[4] and although the segregation of Black and white people in the US has been abolished, the mass incarceration of Black Americans is a growing epidemic.[5] Because we haven't fully identified the deeper psychological drivers and structures of oppression, we've targeted the manifestations of oppression while leaving its core intact, like cutting weeds in a garden while leaving the roots behind to fester and proliferate. When we don't understand the mentality that drives all forms of oppression and the ways this mentality informs social structures, we risk swapping one oppression for another or enabling the same oppression to shapeshift into a new form, even as we work toward transformation.

Understanding the nonrelational mentality that informs all oppressions—and all forms of injustice—not only helps us avoid repeating history but, as I mentioned in Chapter 1, also enables us to more fully and effectively bring about social transformation: it motivates us to unite across causes so that our efforts become greater than the sum of their parts. For example, although we may choose to focus our energy challenging capitalism in order to end global poverty, we can at the same time maintain an awareness of the interconnectedness of capitalism-induced global poverty and other forms of oppression, such as racism, patriarchy, and nonhuman animal exploitation. We can actively raise awareness of the nonrelational mentality, or mindset, that breeds all oppressions so that regardless of the focus of our work for social change, our efforts are contributing to ending oppression more broadly. Each time we choose, for instance, not to call environmentalists who advocate capitalist solutions to end the climate crisis "hypocrites" and instead engage in respectful dialogue to raise their awareness of the role of capitalism in driving climate change, we interrupt the wider pattern of nonrelational thinking and avoid inadvertently reinforcing the very attitudes, behaviors, and policies that create structural inequalities in the first place.[6]

Understanding the nonrelational mentality also enables us to interrupt and shift relationally dysfunctional patterns of thinking and behaving in our personal lives, which is necessary both for the creation of a more just and compassionate world and for our own wellbeing. Because the same attitudes and behaviors that enable social oppression and the oppression of nonhuman animals and the environment also enable interpersonal and even intrapersonal abuse, all levels of oppression or abuse are mutually reinforcing— each feeds the others. When we break the nonrelational pattern on any of these levels and start to build more relational systems, we not only cease reinforcing oppression but also help to transform it. (By including the interpersonal and intrapersonal dimensions, I do not mean to minimize the very real phenomenon of widespread oppression of historically marginalized groups, a point I discuss throughout this book.)

Beyond a Hierarchy of Oppressions

Oppressions often exist alongside—rather than above or below— one another. However, many of us who are working toward social transformation tend to think of oppressions as existing in a competitive hierarchy, with some being more worthy of attention than others. Although it's important from a strategic perspective to consider which cause to prioritize, very often, arguments about prioritization reflect personal value judgments rather than strategic considerations. We tend to view oppressions like rungs on a ladder, and we compete to secure the top position for the oppression about which we are most concerned. As such, we may even assume that one form of oppression underlies all other forms of oppression— thinking, for example, that if patriarchy or class conflict were abolished, then colonialism would topple.[7]

Of course, some oppressions are informed by others. For example, patriarchy gives rise to sexism, heterosexism, and genderism. So patriarchy is the ethos, or backdrop, from which the latter emerge. And some oppressions intersect with others. For instance, patriarchy reinforces and is reinforced by racism and classism, and together, these intersecting oppressions create a distinct social category. What this means is that Black or Brown women are more likely than white women or Black or Brown men to live in poverty, and that the social experience of an economically disadvantaged Black or Brown woman is distinct from that of an economically disadvantaged white woman or a Black or Brown man.[8] This concept of *intersectionality*, previously identified by attorney-activist Kimberlé Crenshaw, is discussed in upcoming chapters.[9]

The assumption that oppressions exist in a competitive hierarchy can limit our effectiveness in working toward social change, as those of us working for different causes can end up fighting against one another in an attempt to claim the top rung of the hierarchical ladder, rather than uniting to abolish the very notion of the ladder, a construct that lies at the heart of all oppression. Of course, I am not suggesting that hierarchies are inherently problematic. Some hierarchies are necessary, such as that between a parent and a child. The problem arises when factors that should not be arranged in a hierarchy—such as moral worth—are.

Although the experiences of the victims of different oppressions vary, the mentality that enables all these oppressions is the same. The same nonrelational mindset that makes it possible for us to tolerate or even support genocides around the world produces and maintains a culture of classist exploitation at home and enables us to justify the confinement of sentient nonhuman animals in factories where their bodies are turned into food. Once we step outside this nonrelational mentality, we can appreciate that oppressions are more like spokes on a wheel than rungs on a ladder, with some select spokes branching out into offshoots, and some intersecting with others.

The Myth of a Hierarchy of Moral Worth

The tendency to think of oppressions hierarchically reflects and reinforces the belief in a hierarchy of moral worth, a concept I introduced in Chapter 1. Although this hierarchy is a myth, most of us don't realize this, and it informs the way we think and feel and, ultimately, the way we relate.

The belief in a hierarchy of moral worth is one reason we don't recognize certain individuals as victims of oppression, even when they are; someone needs to hold a certain moral status in society in order to be recognized as susceptible to victimization. For example, for decades, psychologists noted that girls and women who were forced by familiars to engage in sexual acts (an experience we recognize and refer to today as being sexually assaulted) subsequently exhibited a number of distressing symptoms. However, rather than recognize these symptoms as indicative of trauma—of having been overpowered and controlled—psychologists diagnosed the girls and women as "hysterical," as suffering from personal neuroses.[10] It wasn't until the 1970s, when the women's liberation movement had sufficiently elevated the social and therefore the moral status of girls and women,[11] that such symptoms were recognized as hallmarks of post-traumatic stress disorder (PTSD) and that girls and women were acknowledged as victims of sexual assaults.

The belief in a hierarchy of moral worth is deeply dysfunctional and a key driver of oppression. Oppression drives and is driven by nonrelational dynamics that run counter to the formula for healthy relating, dynamics that violate integrity and harm dignity. Regardless of who another is or what they have done—whether they are our colleague, our family dog, or a convicted murderer— when we view and treat them in a way that denies their dignity, we demean them and violate our core moral values of compassion and justice in the process. Indeed, our psychological, social, and emotional experience is defined and redefined by how we relate— with other humans, with the nonhuman animals with whom we share the planet, and with ourselves. Injuries to our sense of dignity, on the collective and individual levels, lie at the heart of much psychological and relational dysfunction.[12]

When we look at the belief in a hierarchy of moral worth through the lens of psychology, we can see how such a belief is, in fact, inaccurate. We are each nothing more and nothing less than the synthesis of our hardwiring and every momentary experience we've had throughout our lives. Expecting someone to be different from who and how they are is like expecting a tree that's been rained on not to be wet.

Some child abuse survivors, for example, go on to be high achievers and to break the pattern of abuse in their family systems while others do not. Perhaps those in the first group had fewer inherent psychological vulnerabilities, or they had positive role models outside the family or access to information that gave them enough understanding of trauma to be more resilient. Any number of factors could have influenced the experience of members of each group such that the trajectories of their lives shifted in one direction or another. Similarly, some of us go on to be "compassionate" people while others do not; for myriad reasons, those others simply have less access to their compassion. Having just one difficult day— having been stuck in traffic, snapped at by our boss at work, or put on hold for hours—can cause even the most compassionate of us to be less so. So, just as we wouldn't look at a starving person on the street and feel contempt for them because they don't have access to as much food as we do, we shouldn't look down on people who aren't able to access their compassion as much as we are.[13]

Most of us recognize (even if we don't necessarily act accordingly) that we shouldn't use factors such as physical appearance, intelligence, and financial power as criteria to determine whether someone has inherent worth or deserves *moral consideration*—to have their interests be taken into account. However, we have yet to accept that *all* criteria for such a verdict are problematic. This doesn't mean that we shouldn't hold people accountable for their actions. It simply means that we should honor the dignity of all individuals—not judge anyone as more or less worthy of moral consideration—even as we work to change harmful attitudes and behaviors. For example, if we learn of a manager at a company mistreating their coworkers and embezzling money, we may understandably feel anger and want them fired from their position and charged with criminal behavior, but we don't have to perceive them as an inferior being. In other words, we can recognize and respond to problematic behavior without feeling the contempt that signals we've elevated ourselves to a position of moral superiority.

Indeed, contempt is one side of the nonrelational coin. The other side is shame. Shame is the feeling of being less-than—more specifically, of being less worthy than others of being treated with respect. When we feel shame, we feel our dignity's been harmed; we feel we're lacking in inherent worth. Unlike guilt, which reflects how we feel about a behavior, shame reflects how we feel about ourselves, our very being.

Contempt and shame are two of the most disconnecting and harmful of emotions, and they exist only in relationship, only in comparison. We can't, for example, feel less worthy unless there's someone else whom we perceive as more so—even if that "someone" is an idealized version of ourselves. Both these emotions drive and result from nonrelational behaviors. Both exist only when we've bought into the myth of a hierarchy of moral worth. And the antidote to both is the same: empathy for others, and empathy for ourselves. It's impossible to look down on or up at someone if you're looking at the world through their eyes.

The Psychological Roots of Oppression

Although multiple factors, including powerful economic and other institutional forces, give rise to and help maintain oppression, one key factor, which has only recently begun to receive significant attention, is psychology.[14] In many ways, oppression is a psychological phenomenon: the institutions that sustain oppression are created by and for people, and people are psychological beings. And such institutions and other potentially oppressive structures (e.g., norms and traditions) are in large part driven and maintained by the nonrelational mentality and the resulting relational dysfunction.

Most of us recognize relational dysfunction when we see it—for example, between spouses in an unhealthy marriage, or among verbally abusive online commentators. What we typically *don't* realize is that the same dysfunctional dynamics underlie all problematic relationships, including those played out on the societal stage. A spouse who invalidates and dismisses the experience and needs of their partner is engaging in the same type of dysfunction as is an ageist culture that invalidates and dismisses the experiences and needs of older people.

Most of us also recognize relational health when we see it enacted in various personal relationships and social arrangements. Yet we typically don't realize that, for example, a spouse who honors their partner's dignity—who treats their partner as someone who is inherently worthy and therefore deserves to be empathized with, to be treated fairly, and to feel safe[15]—is engaging in the same healthy dynamic as is a society that encourages policies and practices that honor the dignity of members of historically marginalized groups, while also seeking to empower such groups.

Despite the central role that psychology (and, by extension, relationality) plays in enabling oppression, those working toward social transformation rarely give this aspect of the problem the attention it deserves.[16] Instead, discussions about social change have typically centered around ideology and philosophy. Ideological considerations tend to focus on content—on what end, what kind of system, to work toward (e.g., democracy or benevolent dictatorship, capitalism or socialism). Philosophical considerations sometimes also focus on the end, but they address the process, or the means, as well. One critical philosophical consideration is the question of whether an ethical end justifies unethical means: Is it ethical, for instance, to use weapons to create a less violent social order—to try to end oppression using the same tools that helped create the oppression in the first place? Such questions remain unanswered as long as they are not also looked at through the lens of psychology. Approaching ideology or philosophy as devoid of psychology is like approaching language as devoid of grammar. Words alone are not enough to create a coherent and productive conversation.

Ending oppression requires not simply abolishing oppressive policies and practices but transforming the way we think and, ultimately, relate. It requires an understanding of the psychological processes that inform our relationships with ourselves and others so that we can shift from operating, largely unconsciously, within a nonrelational framework to living consciously within one that is healthy and, as such, empowering. This book focuses on illuminating the nonrelational mentality and its manifestations, as well as exploring its alternative, and we'll discuss specific strategies for change in Part 2.

Relationality and Attachment

Although the prevailing assumption among psychologists in many societies, particularly those in the West, has been that healthy psychological functioning requires a high degree of autonomy, this individualistic model has been increasingly challenged. Numerous studies have shown that humans are both inherently and highly relational: we are, for example, hardwired to need connection with others and we're harmed by the experience of disconnection.[17] Indeed, we thrive, both emotionally and neuropsychologically, when we feel connected (and secure) in our relationships; and we are negatively impacted, psychologically and biologically, by affronts to our dignity—by behaviors that deny our inherent worth.

Moreover, fascinating new research on the neuropsychology of attachment suggests that our *attachment style*, the way we attach to others, has a profound impact on many critical aspects of our personal and relational experience: it helps determine our capacity for trust, empathy, and intimacy, as well as our ability to feel secure in (nonthreatening) relationships and within ourselves.[18] In addition, our attachment style influences whether we are attuned to our needs and the needs of others and validate and respond to those needs (when healthful and appropriate); whether we respect our boundaries and the boundaries of others; or whether we tend to be controlling, insensitive, or defensive. Perhaps most notably, our attachment style helps determine our sense of self-worth and our perception of the worth of others, as well as whether or not we honor such worth.

When our attachment style is *insecure*, we are more likely to engage in nonrelational behaviors, directing them toward others and/or allowing others to direct them toward us. We tend to have lower self-worth and therefore to be more defensive against constructive criticism, perceiving it as an affront to our dignity. We tend to feel either inferior or superior to others and to act accordingly. When our attachment style is *secure*, we are more likely to engage in relational behaviors. We have a healthier sense of self-worth, feeling neither superior nor inferior to others, and we tend to be more receptive to information that challenges us to grow.

Although our attachment style is largely the result of our hardwiring and our earliest experiences with our primary caregivers, research suggests that it is also affected and can even be changed by relationships throughout the course of our life.[19] So our attachment style influences and is influenced by others, for better or worse.

And although an actual switch in attachment styles is believed to result from a more prolonged and/or intense relationship, casual interpersonal dynamics, particularly if such dynamics are prevalent—carried out repeatedly and by multiple individuals—may nevertheless push us in one direction or another along the attachment spectrum. Moreover, because neither individuals nor relationships exist in a vacuum, the systems of which we are a part, that are themselves composed of myriad relationships, may play a role in shaping our attachment style.[20]

Looking at a system through the lens of attachment is one way to assess whether the system is healthy or dysfunctional, relational or nonrelational. And it should come as no surprise that oppressive systems are those that cultivate and reflect insecure attachment. Oppressive systems may well create the very conditions—societal, interpersonal, and intrapersonal—that damage a core driver of personal and relational wellbeing: our ability to attach securely.

Oppression and Abuse

Oppression is the unjust allocation and use—the abuse—of power. Societal unjust allocations and abuses of power are usually referred to as "oppression"; interpersonal ones, including those that occur in families, workplaces, and the like, are usually referred to as "abuse." In all cases, however, the dynamic is the same. The same unbalanced allocation and abuse of power that enable oppression also enable abuse. (Similar abusive dynamics can sometimes be carried out intrapersonally. When I refer to interpersonally abusive dynamics in this book, the same points often apply to intrapersonal dynamics, though I won't always note that this is the case.)

However, oppression and abuse are not identical phenomena. Although the psychological processes that underlie the two are often the same, oppression and abuse differ in two key ways.

First, oppression is always systemic—embedded within a system—whereas abuse can be either systemic or an isolated behavior. Many people will occasionally engage in abusive behavior: for example, in the midst of a heated argument, an angry spouse may say things they know will hurt their partner. Although problematic, this kind of behavior is not necessarily part of a pattern that informs a system. In an abusive system, the abuser consistently holds power over the other individual, and this imbalance of power creates a dynamic that mirrors oppressive dynamics.[21] For example, even during so-called "good times," an abusive spouse may still wield power and control over their partner by doing things such as soliciting information about their partner's vulnerabilities to later use against them. In an abusive system, the abuser seeks to maintain and often even grow the power imbalance within the system in order to continue holding power and control over the other; abuse is just a means to that end.[22]

The second difference between oppression and abuse is that unlike abuse, oppression is institutionalized in that it is embraced and maintained by all major social institutions. This is why there is no such thing as "reverse oppression." Oppression, by definition, must be housed within a system in which there is an unjust allocation—an unfair imbalance—of power on the societal level. So, although some women can, for example, act abusively toward men, they cannot *oppress* men because women, as a demographic whole, have less social power than men do.

Often, oppressive dynamics inform abusive ones. Social scientists and social change agents are well aware of how *social power relations*—dynamics between social groups in which one group has more power than does the other, such as men and women— trickle down to influence *interpersonal power relations*, dynamics between individuals in which one individual has more power than the other. For example, in the 1960s, feminists pointed out how institutionalized patriarchy—the socially sanctioned oppression of women and girls that is manifested through sexist attitudes, behaviors, and policies—was a cause of men abusing women in marital relationships. Because both men and women had been conditioned to believe that husbands had the right to control their wives, a number of married men engaged in abusive and controlling behaviors, and their wives didn't recognize such behaviors as abusive but simply accepted them as normal and appropriate.[*][23]

Likewise, when we abuse power interpersonally, we contribute to a broader collective dysfunction, because we as individuals make up broader society. Obviously, the influence of social power relations on interpersonal power relations is far greater than vice versa. However, the process of abusing power on both the societal and interpersonal levels is mutually reinforcing: each feeds the other, and the difference is a matter of degree.

Fortunately, the process of using power in a way that's healthy is also mutually reinforcing on different levels. Understanding the (sometimes subtle) differences between abuse and positive use of power can help us to more fully work toward transformation for ourselves, others, and our world.

---

[*]   I refer to examples of gender-based oppression to demonstrate key concepts and issues. I am aware that historically, many feminists have neglected to address other oppressions, such as racial oppression, and I do not mean to imply that feminism should be without criticism.

3
POWER: THE FORCE OF INJUSTICE

Power over others is weakness disguised as strength.
—Eckhart Tolle

A POWERFUL MAN IS BELIEVED to have said, "Make the lie big, make it simple, keep saying it, and eventually they will believe it."[1] And an even more powerful man is believed to have said, "All through history the way of truth . . . [has] always won. There have been tyrants and murderers . . . but in the end, they always fall. Think of it—always."[2] Both of these individuals were world leaders who used their power to change the course of history. But they were operating from within very different models of power. Hitler, to whom the first quote is attributed, was operating from within a nonrelational model based on dominance and control, whereas Gandhi, the source of the second quote, was operating from within a relational model based on integrity and dignity. One used his power to oppress, the other to liberate.

It is not only world leaders whose power may lead to harm or healing. Each of us is continually engaged in relational dynamics in which our power may be used toward one end or the other. Our beliefs and feelings about power and the way we wield it inform, to a large degree, whether we relate in a way that's functional or dysfunctional. Unfortunately, much of what we've learned about power is unhealthy. The nonrelational systems of which we're a part condition us to support unjust power imbalances and to continually strive to have more power than those on the other side of the power differential. Therefore, understanding how we've been conditioned to think about and relate to our power can help to ensure that we use it to achieve relational health rather than to support the nonrelational status quo.

What Is Power?

Power is the capacity or ability to influence oneself, others, or events to bring about a desired outcome.[3] Basically, when we have power, we're able to exert our will in order to get what we want.

Of course, sometimes, we have power but don't feel powerful.[4] One reason is that we may not be aware of the power we have. For example, even if we have plenty of money, we may also have a "mentality of poverty." So we may not feel financially empowered,[5] meaning that we don't feel that we have the power to take financial action. Another reason we may not feel as powerful as we are is that we have low self-worth—we feel that we don't have sufficient personal value. Indeed, our sense of self-worth can inform, to a significant degree, our perception of our power,[6] as illustrated by the all-too-common example of an individual in a problematic relationship who doesn't feel worthy and, as such, empowered enough to leave. In other words, when our self-worth is low, so too may be our perception of our power and therefore our sense of *empowerment*—our ability to act or influence. Conversely, an inflated sense of self-worth can result in our feeling more powerful than we actually are, such as when, for example, a narcissistic executive behaves recklessly and unethically, thinking they're above reproach.

Moreover, just as our sense of self-worth can influence our perception of our power, so too can our perception of our power influence our sense of self-worth. When we feel that we have the ability to influence ourselves, others, or events, we feel better about ourselves—more worthy. It's also possible to feel powerful in one area of our life but not in another. For example, a CEO of an organization may feel powerful in this role, but may nevertheless lack self-worth and struggle to feel a sense of empowerment in other roles, perhaps as a partner in an intimate relationship.

Power Models

Most social science research on power focuses on two key questions: "How is power exercised or used?" and "For what purpose is it used?" In other words, social scientists are largely interested in the *process*[7] of power, or the *way* that we use and experience our power and the power of others, particularly when we're interacting.[8]

The way that we use and experience power is based on which *power model* we're employing. A power model is a framework or guide for how and why to use our power, including how to increase our sense of empowerment and self-worth—factors that determine, to a large degree, how we relate.

Although social scientists hold a variety of perspectives on power models, these models tend to fall into two categories.[9] One is dysfunctional and disempowering;[10] the other is functional and empowering. One is disconnecting; the other leads to greater connection within ourselves and between ourselves and others.[11] One harms self-worth; the other helps enhance it. One fuels relational dysfunction; the other offsets it.

Essentially, these power models inform the way we relate. They are drivers of nonrelational or relational behaviors.

Social scientists refer to these two power models as the *dominance*, or *power over*, model (for simplicity, I use only "power over" to denote this model) and the *functionalist* model,[12] which is very similar to what some theorists have referred to as the *power with* model (I use the terms "functionalist" and "power with" interchangeably to describe a model that is a hybrid of these two perspectives[13]). And, as with relationality, these power models exist on a spectrum rather than dualistically. So the way that we use and experience power doesn't have to be squarely based on power over or power with, but it can be more or less so.

Power Over

In the power over model, we use our power to exert dominance and control over others, either overtly or subtly. We place our interests above those of others and of the relationships of which we are a part. In other words, we use our power to get what we want, to serve our own ends, without regard for the interests of others. We either apathetically disregard others' interests or intentionally violate them. For example, a stockholder of an oil company may vote against a political initiative to increase support for green energy not because they *want* to harm the environment, but because they don't care about harming it or they care less about the environment than they do about their own profits. Or that same stockholder may vote against such an initiative with the intention to harm a green energy company that's run by a colleague they dislike.

In the power over model, we may also use our power in order to increase our feeling of being powerful by demonstrating to others and/or to ourselves that we have power. (When a feeling or behavior is witnessed, it is validated and can therefore feel more potent.) For example, perhaps the aforementioned stockholder voted against the initiative not to achieve a desirable practical end—more profits—but to demonstrate that they have the power to help block such an initiative, thereby increasing their feeling of being powerful. (I explained in Note 4 how increased levels of dopamine have been associated with the "high" of feeling powerful, such that some researchers have suggested that feeling powerful may be addictive.) In the power over model, we may use our power not simply to feel more powerful but also to feel more worthy. In other words, we sometimes use our power in an attempt to increase our sense of self-worth, often at the expense of others: we may view and treat others as inferior so that we don't feel inferior ourselves.

Social scientists have noted how individuals who feel inferior and ashamed try to defend themselves against acknowledging these feelings by putting others down.[14] Individuals who suffer from narcissistic personality disorder (NPD) are perhaps a prime example of this phenomenon. People with NPD engage in behaviors that are often demeaning to others and they need constant affirmation and adulation because they feel fundamentally unworthy. Indeed, the power over model reflects and reinforces the belief in a hierarchy of moral worth, the central myth driving the nonrelational mentality. We are more likely to use our power at the expense of others when we perceive them as less worthy of moral consideration; and when we use our power at the expense of others, we reinforce the perception that they are in fact less worthy.

When we use power over to feel more worthy, we can end up feeling even less so than we did originally. Imagine, for example, a college student proudly telling his girlfriend (who is also a student) that he got a B on a difficult math exam, and his girlfriend replying with, "I don't know what you're so excited about—it's not like you got an A." He then says, "Well, at least I didn't get a C on my English 101 term paper!" to which his girlfriend retorts, "At least *I* didn't fail an entire semester because I was too depressed to get myself to class!" and so on, in a never-ending cycle of degradation. Eventually, one of the partners will deliver the zinger that hits the other's sense of self-worth hard enough that they back down, likely feeling devastated. For a moment, the winner may feel an inflated sense of power, gloating in their success, but at some point, their guilt will creep in, and they will probably feel ashamed of having demeaned their partner. On some level, the winner knows that succeeding at degrading others is no success at all and that the win-lose model is, in reality, lose-lose.

Indeed, power over is individualistic rather than relational, as power is used to satisfy individual interests without regard for the interests of others or for the greater good of the relationship of which the individuals are a part. Individualistic models tend to be competitive: when people see themselves and their interests as separate from others and from others' interests, they will try to distinguish themselves from others and also try to ensure that their own interests are the ones that get met. For this reason, power over has also been referred to as "competitive power."

On a psychological level, the competitive aspect of power over often manifests through comparison: we feel more or less powerful in some way (beautiful, wealthy, ethical, intelligent, and so on) based on how we compare to others, on how much more or less power we have in a given area than they do.[15] When our sense of self-worth is dependent on factors outside ourselves and often beyond our control, we tend to feel insecure and out of control, whether we realize it or not. And we have to keep searching for more comparisons to keep our self-worth propped up. The power over model is organized around winners and losers, haves and have-nots: one cannot exist without the other, and in this model, we strive to be the former, usually at the expense of others and always at the expense of our integrity. We act against our core moral values of compassion and justice whenever we diminish others. Individualistic models also tend toward dualistic, or all-

or-nothing, thinking. When we perceive ourselves as separate and distinct from others, we tend to think in terms of "either-or" rather than "both-and." We may therefore place individuals and groups into rigid categories in our minds, losing nuance: we see others, and ourselves, as good or bad, right or wrong, a perpetrator or a victim or a hero. We lose the ability to recognize that good people engage in harmful behaviors, and that we can be a perpetrator *and* a victim *and* a hero.

The nonrelational behaviors characteristic of the power over model are inherently disconnecting. We feel disconnected from others when we compete with them and define ourselves as better than they are, because this behavior causes us to be less likely to identify with them (to see something of ourselves in them and something of them in ourselves) and therefore less likely to empathize with them. It is much easier to see someone as a "loser" or a "have-not" when we don't feel what they are feeling. And when our capacity to identify and empathize with another is diminished, so too is our desire and ability to act with compassion. For example, if we perceive our politically conservative sister-in-law as fundamentally different from us, we are more likely to say things to and about her that don't take her feelings into account. So, the power over model causes us to see others as fundamentally different from and inferior to ourselves: it leads to *othering*, which forms the foundation of prejudice.[16] Moreover, when we participate in power over dynamics intrapersonally, we feel disconnected from ourselves. When we engage in self-degradation, telling ourselves we're "stupid" or "lazy," we're empathizing with ourselves less, and we therefore feel less compassion for ourselves. We also feel disconnected from ourselves because when we exercise power over, we act against the formula for healthy relating, as we (in most cases) violate our integrity—we disconnect from our core values.

Physical and Psychological Power Over

In its extreme expression, power over reflects the dynamics of domination and subjugation. Consider, for example, the dynamics of rape, genocide, slavery, and nonhuman animal exploitation. All power and control have been taken from those being victimized. This results in their physical disempowerment, or lack of ability to act or influence, and in some cases in their psychological disempowerment, or lack of *belief* in their ability to act or influence.[17] Psychological disempowerment often, though not always, also includes a diminished sense of self-worth. When we exercise physical power over another, we use physical means or practical means such as money to overpower or control them, rendering them disempowered. When we exercise psychological power over another, we use psychological means toward the same end, often by getting them to distrust their own perceptions, to question the truth of their experience—in essence to get them to see themself through our eyes and to trust our perceptions over their own. As a result, their sense of self-control, confidence, and (as noted) often self-worth are replaced with self-doubt, insecurity, and shame.

Even when power over is expressed primarily through physical means, it nearly always causes some degree of psychological disempowerment as well. For example, it's almost impossible for someone being raped to resist internalizing the message that they are not worthy of respect as their body is being overpowered and violated.[18] Moreover, psychologically disempowering someone who's being victimized is usually a necessary prerequisite for obtaining full power and control over them.[19] People's automatic impulse is to resist being overpowered and controlled, so they must be coerced into participating in their own oppression, often by being convinced that they are not worthy of being treated justly.

For example, many cult leaders convince their followers to distrust their own perceptions and feelings and to believe that their self-worth comes from acting in accordance with the dictates of the cult.[20] So the cult members are far more receptive to being physically controlled and they are less likely to resist being treated harshly for deviating from the rules. (Individuals are in no way responsible for their victimization, but the process of victimization often causes them to unwittingly act against their own interests.)

Sometimes, behaviors that reflect the power over model are not enacted in order to demean or otherwise cause unnecessary harm but are simply the result of automatic responses to stimuli, most notably when the prefrontal cortex, the region of the brain that enables us to make rational decisions, has been bypassed. In these cases, our behaviors are the result of neurochemical reactions that are not in our control, such as when we're reacting to an immediate threat to our physical safety or because of a condition such as post-traumatic stress disorder (PTSD). Indeed, the human brain is hardwired to engage in such behaviors when necessary, and these behaviors have performed an important evolutionary function, helping preserve the wellbeing of groups, communities, and humanity by ensuring that potential threats to oneself or one's group are readily perceived and reacted to.

Functionalist social scientists, such as Dacher Kelter, author of *The Power Paradox*, point out that although power over behaviors in humans were once necessary for survival, today, given the evolution of complex social organization and social intelligence, such behaviors are largely dysfunctional.[21] Looking at the construction of leadership, they note how in complex modern societies, lasting power must be earned rather than taken by brute force. Power is not bestowed upon those who dominate but rather given to those who build relationships within the group, advancing the interests of all group members. Of course, corrupt leaders exist, and power can corrupt even the most ethical leaders. And, as noted, behaviors that reflect the power over model are to some degree hardwired. However, functionalist social scientists hold that such behaviors tend to harm groups rather than protect and preserve them. Moreover, given the development of human social intelligence, we are no longer fully at the mercy of our automatic reactions; we can make conscious, intentional choices about how to act, rather than operate on instinct. We have evolved to also be able to make choices that reflect long-term considerations rather than a short-sighted drive for instant gratification. Human and planetary wellbeing depends on behaviors that serve not merely the interests of the individual but the interests of all stakeholders and, ultimately, the greater good of the group or relationship. These behaviors are reflected and reinforced by the relational power with model.

Power With (The Functionalist Model)

Unlike the nonrelational power over model, which reflects and reinforces the belief in a hierarchy of moral worth, the relational power with model reflects and reinforces the belief that all individuals possess equal inherent worth—the same essential dignity. As such, all individuals are recognized as equally deserving of moral consideration.

In the power with model, power is used in the service of the whole—for the greater good of the relationship or group. Behaviors that reflect this model foster connection, enhanced self-worth, and mutual relational empowerment[22] (the ability to act or influence in ways that are relationally healthful). In the power with model, when we use our power, we take into account the impact of our choices on others and act in the best interests of the whole. We strengthen our sense of empowerment and self-worth by helping others strengthen theirs. We therefore feel more connected with others—psychologically, because we identify with them, and emotionally, because we empathize with them. And we feel more connected with ourselves, both because we self-empathize more and because when we act in accordance with our core moral values, we feel more internal unity—our values and practices are more aligned.

Indeed, the power with model is organized around practicing integrity and honoring dignity—that is, practicing the formula for healthy relating. Acting in the best interests of all parties requires the behaviors that foster trust, security, connection, and awareness.

As mentioned in Chapter 1, the core moral values integrity is based on include, most notably, compassion and justice.[23] Practicing these values is supported by practicing curiosity, honesty, and courage. *Compassion* is having an open heart and truly caring about the wellbeing of others and of ourselves—and, furthermore, acting on that caring, such as when a competitive sibling chooses to praise his brother's achievements or when "ordinary" people come together in the aftermath of a natural disaster to provide relief for those in need. *Justice* is doing to others as we would have others do to us, and treating them as we imagine they would want to be treated, given what we understand of them—and vice versa, for those of us who tend to treat others better than we treat ourselves. *Curiosity* is having an open mind, genuinely seeking understanding—such as when arguing partners pause and truly hear each other's point of view or if the dominant white culture in the United States were to listen to and acknowledge the claims of Indigenous Americans, whose voices have been silenced and whose history has been largely erased. *Honesty* is not simply telling the truth but also seeing the truth. Honesty is not denying or avoiding important truths, even if those truths are painful to face—such as when a parent opens their eyes to the reality that their child is addicted to drugs or when Germans acknowledged the genocide perpetrated in their name and constructed programs and policies to help prevent history from repeating itself. *Courage* is bravery, which includes the willingness to be honest and curious, even when doing so feels frightening or threatening; it is the willingness to be vulnerable with others and with ourselves.

When we practice integrity by acting out these core values (and we honor dignity by perceiving as well as treating others as worthy of our practicing integrity), it is usually, if not always, an all-win situation. What enhances, or boosts, my level of integrity helps you enhance yours. What enhances the integrity of a relationship helps enhance the integrity of everyone in that relationship. And when each individual practices integrity, the integrity of the world is enhanced. So a useful guiding question when making any kind of relational or social decision is, "What would enhance my integrity?" or "What would enhance the integrity of the relationship or the world?" For example, perhaps a group of men is making sexist comments about some women colleagues, discussing the women's bodies or sexuality, and you speak up to interrupt the process of power over. Pointing out the sexist behavior reinforces your integrity and encourages others to practice theirs. It also helps enhance integrity on the societal level, because you've disrupted problematic patriarchal attitudes and behaviors.

When we engage in the relational behaviors that reflect the power with model, we are essentially practicing our integrity by making it easier for others to practice theirs. And, as is the case with power over, this creates a feedback loop: the more we practice integrity, the more we increase the chances that we, and others, will continue to be relational rather than dysfunctional.

Relational behaviors constitute the practice of love. In his seminal book *The Road Less Traveled*, psychiatrist M. Scott Peck contends that love is not merely a feeling—it is also an action.[24] Peck says that the behavior of love is acting in the best interests of another, which is essentially practicing integrity.

Engaging in relational behaviors ultimately helps us evolve toward our highest selves, in large part because it helps bring us into a state of presence. When we are in this state, we are present in the moment. We don't ruminate about the future or lament the past; rather, we mindfully direct our awareness toward our own current, unfolding experience and that of others. We feel connected with others and ourselves through our sense of empathy and compassion—through a recognition of our shared mortality and capacity for suffering, as well as our shared dignity.[25] This state of presence is what many of the most renowned philosophers, spiritual teachers, and psychologists refer to as our ideal and most highly evolved state.

Shame and Contempt Versus Pride and Humility

In Chapter 2, we discussed how shame and contempt are two of the most nonrelational of emotions and how they drive and result from nonrelational behaviors. Shame, as we discussed, is the feeling of being less inherently worthy than others, while contempt is the feeling of being more worthy than others. So it should come as no surprise that the power over model is a major driver of shame and contempt.

Shame both results from and causes many of the nonrelational behaviors that reflect the power over model and that violate integrity and harm dignity, in a vicious cycle. When we feel shame, we are less likely to pay attention to and practice integrity because our focus is on self-defense, on preventing ourselves from feeling even more ashamed. Shame can make us feel as though we're drowning emotionally, so we grab for anything that floats, often pushing others under in the process. Imagine, for example, that a young man who has recently started dating another man reveals to his new romantic interest that his feelings are growing and that he wants to make a more serious commitment. The other, however, expresses some ambivalence and asks for more time to consider what direction he would like the relationship to go in. The first man may feel rejected and therefore ashamed. He may be tempted to avoid the other's phone calls or to make it clear that he's actively pursuing other potential love interests. These actions are designed to protect his sense of self-worth—possibly even to make the other man question his, so that the young man feels more worthy by comparison.

Shame is arguably the foundation of human psychological dysfunction and, by extension, social dysfunction.[26] To feel worthy is a powerful, essential human need, and shame is so disruptive to our psychological security and wellbeing that we often will do just about anything to avoid this feeling. We may accumulate millions of dollars, sculpt our physical image to fit a cultural ideal of beauty, or strive to become a paragon of success in the areas that matter to us, possibly even at the expense of others.[27] Indeed, wars have been waged in defense of honor—that is, in an attempt to offset shame—and in some cultures, suicide is considered a better alternative to having one's shame exposed.

To feel shame is to feel that the core of who we are is flawed, not good enough, invalid. And because feeling shame is itself shameful (we feel ashamed of being ashamed), we tend to hide our shame from others and even from ourselves. We pretend it doesn't exist. We bury it under endless piles of work, wrap it inside our achievements, and tuck it away beneath the layers of distractions that continuously keep our focus outside ourselves. We act as if we feel like we're good enough, perhaps even superior, when inside we are self-doubting and feeling like an imposter. In relationships, we act as if we don't care and withhold words of affection, when what we really want is for the other to tell us how much they love us.

Shame is also a powerful means of social control. Members of groups with less social power are often conditioned to feel ashamed of their situation and of themselves for being in it, rather than to feel the motivating emotion of anger, which would be a more appropriate reaction to the injustice of their circumstances. For example, North Americans whose first language is English often raise their voices in frustration when speaking with nonnative English-speaking immigrants who don't understand what they're saying, as though the immigrants were unable to hear properly rather than struggling against a language barrier. Meanwhile, the immigrants frequently feel ashamed of themselves for not understanding the native English speakers, believing that the latter's annoyance is justified and that any misunderstandings are due to their own shortcomings—to their lack of English proficiency. More likely, though, such communication breakdown is caused by the (probably monolingual) native speakers, who lack an understanding of the appropriate means of communicating with nonnative speakers. It's also likely that the native speakers' irritation and raised voices reflect not justifiable anger but disrespect, probably stemming from racism and/or nationalism. Were the immigrants to realize these facts and to appreciate that they have an equal right to occupy the same space as the native English-speaking North Americans (whose families were most likely immigrants themselves at some point, generations ago), their shame would no doubt be replaced by anger.

Shaming others is a counterproductive means of encouraging positive change in their attitudes and behaviors. Indeed, research has demonstrated that people typically respond to being shamed by engaging in defensive dynamics; they are less likely to think rationally and act compassionately and are more likely to act in ways that are nonrelational.[28] So if we want people to respond to requests or even demands for positive change, we need to communicate in a way that honors their dignity, while still raising awareness of the problems they've caused and holding them accountable. Of course, some people, in some situations, respond to being shamed by making positive changes. However, it's likely that they responded in such a way *in spite* of, rather than *because* of, having been shamed. Moreover, people can feel ashamed even when they're not being shamed, but this doesn't negate the importance of avoiding the use of shame as a tactic to encourage positive change.

It can be challenging to avoid shaming. Evolutionary psychologists have noted that historically, shame has been used to ensure that members of communities adhered to social norms and values, to keep tribes and societies intact. When people act in ways that are antithetical to social norms by, for example, abusing drugs or engaging in what's considered inappropriate sexual activity, they get the message that they're "wrong" and deserve to be punished or rejected. Social norms cause us to feel compelled to shame others, and to have a strong reaction to being shamed ourselves.

There are a handful of studies that appear to support shame as a positive change strategy. However, when you read these studies more closely, they are not contradicting what the rest of the literature on shame says.[29] The difference is generally one of context or semantics. In writings where authors claim that "punching up"—attacking someone in a position of greater power, generally in order to bring about justice—will ultimately end injustice, there is also a lack of understanding of the psychological and relational dynamics that both drive and result from shame.[30]

Psychologists point out that grandiosity is frequently a mask for shame. Grandiosity, like contempt, is the sense of superiority.

However, unlike contempt, grandiosity doesn't necessarily include disdain for others, though it certainly can. Grandiosity is the feeling that we're more powerful than we actually are, which may or may not entail feeling more worthy of being treated with respect than others. Regarding grandiosity, consider a person who's high on drugs or who's got a chemical imbalance in their brain whereby they believe they can jump off a building or drive recklessly without getting hurt. Regarding contempt, consider a boy who falls down on the playground and is teased (shamed) for crying over his scraped knee. He pulls himself up, puffs out his chest, and punches at his bullies in an "I'll show you" display of force. The shamed becomes the shamer, perpetuating a cycle that is unfortunately a hallmark of many interactions and relationships. Or consider how some working-class white people who feel inferior compared to their more educated or financially advantaged counterparts may degrade and bully Black and Brown people, who appear as a convenient "other" against whom they may position themselves as superior.

Indeed, beneath all our striving to feel powerful, in control, beautiful, successful, and so on, what we each truly want is to feel that we are enough, that we are worthy. We want to feel that regardless of what we do, it is who we are intrinsically that matters. We want to feel pride. Healthy pride is not the expression of an inflated ego but rather the recognition that we are fundamentally worthy. Pride is feeling not less worthy than, but as worthy as others. Pride is the opposite of shame. It is the essence of personal and social wellbeing, just as shame is the foundation of personal and social dysfunction. Pride motivates us to take positive action on behalf of ourselves and others. This is one reason why social justice movements often seek to cultivate pride in those they represent and support. For example, in the US, in the 1960s and 1970s (and again in more recent years, with movements like Black Girl

Magic and Black Lives Matter), the Black pride movement sought to transform the internal experience of Black people so that they would feel empowered to demand transformation of the external power structures that oppressed them.

Perhaps not surprisingly, the power with model helps transform shame into pride. Shame is incompatible with integrity, and engaging in healthy, relational behaviors enhances integrity. Integrity brings us into connection with others, ourselves, and our values. One indication that we are in a healthy dynamic is that we feel an absence or alleviation of shame. And just as pride is the opposite of shame, humility is the opposite of grandiosity (and contempt). Humility is the recognition that we are not more worthy than others but (as with pride) as worthy as they are. When we are both proud and humble, we recognize our own worth and appreciate the worth of others. We recognize the inherent worth of other beings with whom we share the planet, and our practices and policies reflect this understanding.

Unlike shame and grandiosity/contempt, which exist only in relationship as they're based on comparison, pride and humility can exist independent of a relationship, as they're not based on comparison. These emotions can, however, be inspired by healthy, relational interactions.

Trauma and Addiction Versus Presence and Love

The power over model informs the dynamics of trauma—of perpetrator and victim (and sometimes hero). People become traumatized when they feel victimized, when they feel powerless to control a situation in which they are under threat physically or emotionally.[31] People can also become traumatized when they witness a traumatic event and feel powerless to control the outcome. Trauma causes us to lose connection with ourselves and others and, of course, to lose our sense of security. Traumatized individuals feel disconnected and insecure internally and externally.[32] Traumatic events also cause and reflect shame and grandiosity. Individuals who have been victimized often experience shame, while perpetrators are frequently in a state of grandiosity; each role and feeling feed the other.

The power over model also informs the dynamics of addiction. An addicted person feels powerless and disempowered. They are also victimized by the addiction: the object of their addiction has total power and control over them, and the experience of addiction is often traumatic for them and for others in their life as well.

Four drivers of addiction are the feelings of disconnection, insecurity, disempowerment, and low self-worth. Addictive behaviors often create a temporary feeling of connection (i.e., a "oneness" or "unity" within oneself and with others) and security, as well as of empowerment and worthiness. However, once the high (from drinking, gambling, sex, etc.) wears off, the problematic feelings often actually intensify.

An individual who suffers from addiction also experiences both shame and grandiosity. On one level, they often feel profound shame for their sense of powerlessness to control their own behaviors. At the same time, their "inner addict," the part of their psyche that drives them to maintain the addiction, may make them believe that they are in control of something they actually have no control over, so they perceive themself as more powerful than they actually are.

Trauma and addiction are two sides of the power over coin: they are both expressions of the nonrelational dynamics of power over, and they tend to reinforce each other. It is no coincidence that many people who have been traumatized also suffer from addiction.

By contrast, the relational dynamics of power with are, ultimately, the dynamics of presence and love. Presence is essentially the opposite of trauma and addiction. It is a state of connection and nonviolence, whereas trauma results from and causes disconnection and violence. And although engaging in an addictive behavior creates a *sense* of connection, making us feel temporarily unified with others and ourselves, it is ultimately disconnecting. Moreover, presence is also a state of acceptance and awareness, whereas addiction is a state of craving that relies on self-delusion for its fulfillment.

When we are in a state of addiction, we are focused on one thing: gratification from the addictive "fix," be it alcohol, working, or our own self-perception. We may use any means necessary toward this end, even if it involves violating our integrity, which it often does. When we are in a state of presence, however, we are not attached to an identity or ego, nor to an outcome that we try to control, so we are able to be open to and connected with what are perhaps the deepest aspects of ourselves and others: our shared mortality and dignity. We are therefore able to express and receive love in perhaps the truest sense of the word.

4
NONRELATIONAL SYSTEMS: THE ARCHITECTURE OF INJUSTICE

It is no measure of health to be well adjusted
to a profoundly sick society.
—Jiddu Krishnamurti (attributed)

IN 1633, THE RENOWNED MATHEMATICIAN Galileo Galilei was convicted of heresy. He was placed under house arrest for the rest of his life, and it was forbidden that he or others publish any of his future works. His crime? Supporting the theory of his predecessor Copernicus, who'd argued that the planets revolved around the sun. The prevailing belief was that the planets revolved around Earth, the exalted center of the universe. To proclaim otherwise, even when such an assertion was supported by sound mathematical calculations, was not only to call into question the validity of established scientific and religious assumptions but also to expose the fact that these assumptions were based on a dogmatic and irrational belief system. Such a system is unable to stand up to scrutiny, so it depends on its proponents to deny, condemn, and even kill in order to maintain its status quo.

Since then, social scientists have long demonstrated the power of systems, including entrenched belief systems, to influence human psychology and social behavior. However, widespread ignorance and denial of the impact of systems persist, which is a key reason why nonrelational systems continue unchecked. Were we to truly appreciate how systems shape our lives and world, we would be better able to challenge those systems that turn random or isolated nonrelational behaviors into widespread, institutionalized oppression (and that enable ongoing abuse).

Indeed, although nonrelational dynamics inform nonrelational systems, for such systems to manifest fully, the dynamics need a vehicle, a structure or framework through which they may be more fully incorporated into a society or relationship. In other words, *nonrelationality* needs a system to house, legitimize and disseminate it. It is the combination of nonrelational dynamics with a system that gives rise to oppressive systems (and, to a lesser degree, abusive systems).

Systems:
The Dances That Shape Our Lives and Our World

A system is a set of interconnected parts that form a whole, which, as systems psychologist Harriet Lerner points out, is similar to a dance.[1] A dance is made up of dancers, music, and dance steps, and the way these parts come together creates the whole, integrated ensemble. In some dances, we feel insecure and self-conscious; in others, we feel confident and inspired. In some dances, we have our toes stepped on and are forced to follow someone else's lead even if we don't want to; in others, we and they move gracefully together as true partners.

Some systems to which we belong include just one other person, as with a couple system, whereas some include millions of others, as with social systems. When a system involves only two people, we usually refer to it simply as a "relationship." Larger systems are essentially sets of relationships. We even have an internal system: according to one psychological model, our personality is not one cohesive whole but comprises multiple parts, or personalities, that are always interacting with one another, for better or worse.[2]

Like a dance, each system has its own personality. The personality of a system is made up of the personalities and behaviors of the people in it, as well as the way these individuals interact or come together. A family, for example, is more than just the composite of its members. The way that all those members interact creates the particular personality of the family as a whole. Families can be fun-loving and spontaneous, serious and deliberate, supportive and loving, abusive and dysfunctional, and so on.

The parts of a system include its participants (people, nonhuman animals, and in some cases, nature) with certain roles to play, and rules or guidelines that dictate how the participants should behave and experience themselves and others in their roles. Any role or rule in a given system can be *explicit* (stated aloud or otherwise consciously acknowledged) or *implicit* (unstated and therefore often unconsciously understood).

Although many of the roles we play in systems are explicit—such as that of father, sister, manager, or chairperson—most are implicit. For example, in a personal relationship, we may be the "underfunctioner" when we struggle to maintain our responsibilities, or we may be the "overfunctioner" when we take on the responsibilities of the other person, who is underfunctioning. Or, on the social stage, we may be the "rational, impartial moderate" when we speak on behalf of an established social system, or the "emotional, biased radical" when we challenge that system.

As with roles, some rules are explicit, such as "no swearing in the house" or "no sexual relations outside the marriage," but most are implicit, such as "nobody talks about Mom's drinking." And it may be implicitly understood that the overfunctioner makes the important decisions for the couple, or that the person challenging the established social system is not to be taken seriously.

Many of the most powerful systems in our lives are those whose roles and rules we've never overtly learned but unconsciously and fully integrated into our experience. We step to songs we don't hear with partners we don't see, keeping alive dances we might otherwise choose to end. For example, someone may be well into their middle years before realizing that they've been playing the role of "caretaker" their entire life—that many of their relationships have been with people whose needs they took care of, to the detriment of their own. Or it may be only after someone's adult child comes out as gay that they realize they've been perpetuating prejudice and discrimination through their attitudes and behaviors.

Social scientists have noted two key types of systems: open and closed. An open system is open to change; a closed system is closed or resistant to change. Of course, like most phenomena, systems exist on a spectrum, so a system can be more or less open or closed.

In an open system, roles can change, and rules are fluid. Roles and expectations shift as situations change and/or members of the system grow. For example, in a family system, if the provider loses their job, rather than collude in judgment and shaming, the family responds supportively, with compassionate and reflective understanding and perhaps by rearranging the family structure so that another person willingly takes on the role of provider. Likewise, when a person in a wheelchair points out that the design of their workplace doesn't meet their needs, they are heard, validated, and attended to rather than framed as controlling—as trying to impose their needs on others.

In a closed system, roles and rules are rigid and unchanging. Closed systems seek to maintain the status quo, the way things are, even if everyone involved is miserable. Many of us know a couple who are spectacularly unhappy in their relationship yet stay together because each partner has a long list of reasons why any change would be impossible. Closed systems force conformity: either we conform to the roles and rules of the system, or we are forced out. If, for example, everyone at the company we're employed by chronically overworks and we also overwork, we'll be accepted and celebrated. If we choose not to conform to this expectation, chances are high that we'll be seen as uncommitted and that we'll end up either being fired or wanting to quit.

Sometimes, closed systems appear to be changing when, in fact, they are not; they're just reconfiguring themselves. For example, in a couple relationship, when the person playing the role of "distancer" changes their tune and starts pursuing greater intimacy, the other person, who has been playing the role of "pursuer," may suddenly get cold feet and start distancing (which often makes the former pursue even more). So the pursuer–distancer system doesn't really change at all: the partners simply swap roles, and the original dynamic and level of intimacy stay in place.[3] Or when members of groups with less social power are finally granted access to more power, they may find that that access is largely fraudulent. For instance, the "sexual revolution" of the 1970s enabled women to break out of their traditional gender role, which had placed their value almost entirely on their ability to provide for men in the domestic arena and which had limited their freedom of sexual expression. However, with their newfound sexual liberation came the expectation not that they would stop being domestic providers, but that they would also be sexual providers. So women became domestically and sexually objectified.[4] Neither situation honored women as inherently worthy or truly afforded them the opportunity to grow beyond roles that served to maintain the patriarchal status quo.

Perhaps not surprisingly, open systems tend to be those that are relational, and closed systems tend to be nonrelational.

Nonrelational Systems

Nonrelational systems, as mentioned in Chapter 1, are oppressive or abusive systems, and they're organized around the belief in a hierarchy of moral worth. They are characterized by an unjust imbalance of power among the groups or individuals in them, and they are structured in such a way as to maintain—and often even to grow—this power imbalance. Indeed, the whole structure of a nonrelational system ensures that power never balances out. (Systems that simply have an imbalance of power but are not based on a hierarchy of moral worth, such as that of a parent and a child, are not necessarily nonrelational.) By contrast, relational systems, which are organized around integrity and dignity, may become increasingly balanced in the distribution of power as they evolve.

A continual increase in a power imbalance is often a hallmark of any system in which one individual or group exercises power over others, even if the nonrelational dynamics are so subtle as to be undetectable. Subtle nonrelational dynamics can take many forms: indirect criticism (e.g., a white Briton asking someone of Asian descent where they're "really" from, thinking this constitutes polite small talk but indirectly implying that the listener doesn't belong in the UK); withdrawal (e.g., refusing to engage in a conversation that isn't in the interest of the individual or group with more power); internal criticism (e.g., degrading and shaming oneself in one's internal dialogue); and projection (e.g., framing feminists as angry man-haters, thereby creating negative stereotypes about a social group that challenges an oppressive system). With each repetition of the nonrelational dynamic, the system is bolstered and the power imbalance is maintained or increased.

As with all systems, a nonrelational system can involve as few as two participants or as many as millions of participants. On the interpersonal level, these are often abusive dyadic relationships, family systems, or work cultures.[5] On the societal level, they are oppressive systems, sometimes referred to as "systems of oppression."[6] Examples of these large-scale systems include racism, sexism, and classism, all of which have a structure that ensures that groups with social power remain in power and that the dominant way of relating remains nonrelational.

Oppressive systems are often *dominant systems*, meaning they are so widespread that their tenets are seen as universal truths—the way things are and the way things are meant to be—rather than as a set of widely held opinions. They are invisible, woven into the fabric of society to shape norms, laws, beliefs, behaviors, and so on. These systems impact (and create) many of our deeply held beliefs, and they influence everything from whose opinions we take more seriously to whose needs we perceive as more valid and whose version of history we teach our children. Some historians, for instance, have pointed out that the gender bias in the mainstream version of history makes it truly "*his* story" and that a more objective, fact-based analysis of history shows a very different picture of human nature and gender from what we have been led to believe.[7] When a social system is oppressive, its impact extends to virtually all of our interactions, with strangers and with those with whom we share our most intimate selves. However, because most of us are not conscious of the fact that we are being influenced in such a way, we unknowingly bring these nonrelational dynamics into our hearts and homes, where they can wreak havoc on our lives and damage our relationships and where we may recreate and reinforce them, even as we work to transform these same systems on the societal level.

Each oppressive system is organized around a central belief—a myth—that a particular type of individual is more worthy than others, and the system justifies such a belief by valuing the supposedly inherent qualities of that type of individual over the supposedly inherent qualities of others.[8] One way to see the values espoused by each oppressive system is to look at the terminology associated with the opposing groups within it. We tell boys and men, for instance, to "man up" or to "act like a man" when we want them to "improve" themselves or their behavior. We associate masculinity with strength (defined as the ability not to be emotional or vulnerable, characteristics seen as "feminine"), rationality, independence, and authority. Conversely, we associate girls and women and femininity with emotionality and irrationality, dependence, and fragility. Indeed, whereas there are scant few terms that degrade girls and women for being like boys or men (and these terms, like "tomboy" or "butch," can be neutral or simply relevant to sexual orientation and don't necessarily reflect poorly on masculinity), the most degrading terms to apply to a boy or man are those that mark him as female. For instance, we denigrate boys and men by calling them "sissies," "pussies," and "bitches" and by telling them they throw (or run) "like a girl." "Girl" and "woman," when applied to boys and men, are actually insults. (Imagine the impact on the psyches of girls and women when their very gender, a central feature of who they are, represents the most despised and shameful way to be.) Similarly, we use a range of positive descriptors for "white," such as "pure," "clean," and "good," while the opposite holds true for "black." We don't get punished for telling white lies, which aren't so bad, while we get "blacklisted" if we've done something that really is bad. Unless we are explicitly educated about the nature and structure of oppressive systems, we simply assume, for example, that it is preferable to be rational rather than emotional (moreover, that these qualities cannot coexist), or that men are emotionally stronger than women and boys have more value than girls.

Because the overarching myth, or *metamyth*, of all nonrelational systems is the myth of a hierarchy of moral worth, one could argue that all oppressive systems are subideologies of a single *metasystem*: nonrelationality, the overarching system informing how all oppressive and abusive systems operate. Nonrelationality is the ethos; it is the hub of the wheel from which all the spokes radiate.[9]

Oppressive systems are also interlocking, in that they overlap with and reinforce one another, as we discussed in Chapter 2.[10] Take, for example, the concept of "successful aging," a myth that dominates the field of (Western) gerontology and that reflects and reinforces not only ageism but also a variety of other interlocking oppressions.[11] Critics of this model point out that successful aging, which entails retaining the qualities and features of youth, essentially means *not aging* and therefore negates the inherent value of members of older age groups. They point out that this myth sets us all up to fail, as none of us can actually not age.[12] Moreover, the successful-aging model is classist, because in order to feel—or "pass as"—younger, we must have the socioeconomic means to do so: we must have access to, for instance, quality healthcare and nutrition. The model is ableist as well, as it suggests that the development of a disability—such as not being able to hear—amounts to failure.[13] And it perpetuates heterosexist and sexist norms of, for example, the virile man and attractive woman, whose beauty is equated with both youth and personal worth.[14] In short, individual oppressions, such as ageism or ableism, tailor the metamyth to target individuals of particular demographics (such as older people or people with disabilities). And these systems also interlock, with each oppression and each myth reinforcing the others.

Power Roles and Rules

Nonrelational systems create power roles, or roles based on an unequal distribution of power. In an interpersonal relationship, the *powerholder*—the individual with more power—may be, for instance, the "abuser," or the controlling partner. In social systems, the role we play is determined by the social group or groups to which we belong. Our social group membership is based on such factors as race, gender, social class, sexual orientation, ideology, and even species. So, for example, our role may be "white," "Black," or "Brown"; "man," "woman," or "genderqueer"; "poor," "working class," or "upper class"; "heterosexual," "homosexual," or "asexual"; "young" or "old"; even "human" or "animal."[15] And because systems are interlocking, our power role, such as that of a "Brown working-class woman," can reflect multiple groups at once. Social scientists refer to these different social groups as "dominant" and "nondominant."[16]

Members of dominant groups have too much power, whereas members of nondominant groups have too little power, and this uneven distribution perpetuates the unjust power imbalances that result from nonrelational systems. For example, research has shown that the vast majority of white Americans harbor racist attitudes, either overtly or subtly.[17] So, members of the dominant white group, who hold significantly more social power than do members of the nondominant, "non-white" group, often support legislation and policies that inevitably reinforce racism.

Nonrelational systems create and perpetuate rules to ensure that everyone continues playing their roles so that the status quo of the system is maintained. These rules encourage people to do the very things that prevent power from balancing out, rendering the systems self-perpetuating. The more everyone follows the rules and therefore plays their prescribed roles, the more they reinforce the idea that such rules are legitimate and the more fixed they become in the roles. For example, one rule of patriarchy is that boys and men should be dominant and active, while girls and women should be subordinate and passive, and studies have shown that teachers are more likely to encourage and reward dominance in boys and therefore to engender passivity in girls.[18] And the more that men and women identify with and play out the roles of "dominant male" and "submissive female," the more that traditional gender roles and power imbalances are reinforced—and the more the tenets of patriarchy are legitimized. One way that these gender roles get played out is by women responding to men who take up space by making themselves smaller to take up less space—either physically, sitting with their legs crossed, or symbolically, ceding the floor to men in mixed-gender discussion groups or allowing their male domestic partners to set the emotional tone for their relationships (when he's happy, she's happy, and when he's not, neither is she). As men take up more space, women take up less, and as women take up less space, men take up more.

Specifically, a nonrelational system's rules reward conformity and punish deviation, and they are often expressed as *paths of least resistance*, a concept used by sociologist Allan G. Johnson to explain how dominant groups maintain social power in oppressive systems (but which is applicable to abusive systems as well).[19] Paths of least resistance are ways of thinking and behaving that conform to the beliefs and values of a given system—they constitute the "easy" way to be. Going against the path of least resistance takes effort and often comes with a cost. For example, if a young man is with a group of men friends who happen to be making degrading jokes about women, it is far easier for him to laugh along with them than to call them out on their behavior and risk being taunted himself. Or, in a relationship with the implicit rule that only the powerholding partner is allowed to feel and express anger toward the other partner, usually both partners automatically go along with this entitlement. Anger about or directed toward powerholders is a threat to nonrelational systems, an issue we'll discuss further in Chapter 5.[20] Indeed, what is stated explicitly is often actually contradictory to such a rule. Consider, for example, the following scenario between an abusive mother and her teenage son: The mother asks her son, who seems unhappy, what's wrong, encouraging him to open up and share what's bothering him. The son admits that since his mother started a new job and has been coming home late at night, he hasn't been sleeping well and is feeling frustrated with her for not being quieter. The mother becomes offended and defensive; she attacks him, arguing that he's too light of a sleeper. Or she withdraws to sulk in self-pity, telling her son he doesn't appreciate how hard she works and how much she sacrifices for him, guilting him into apologizing and retracting his statement. When a non-powerholder expresses anger at a powerholder, it's sometimes accompanied by a request that the powerholder change a nonrelational behavior, a request that tends to be met with resistance and attempts to maintain the nonrelational norm.

The Three Defenses of Nonrelational Systems

Nonrelational systems—both social and interpersonal—are organized around a set of falsehoods, or myths,[21] that reflect the opinions of those with more power but that just about everyone buys into. These myths are expressed through *cognitive distortions*,[22] such as denial and justification, and *narratives*, which are stories that reflect the cognitive distortions and are woven together to create an even stronger defensive structure. The myths are sustained on a practical level through *privileges* that give some individuals or groups more power than others. Cognitive distortions, narratives, and privileges are the three key defenses of nonrelational systems, and they interact with one another to maintain these systems. The three defenses are explained in detail in Chapters 5, 6, and 7.

Moreover, the roles and rules of nonrelational systems reinforce the three defenses, and vice versa, in a feedback loop: the more we play the roles and follow the rules, the more we validate the myths (distortions and narratives) and the more we legitimize the privileges granted to those with more power. In turn, our validating myths and legitimizing privileges reinforce our identification with our roles and increase the probability that we will play by the rules of the system. For example, in a heterosexist system, the roles we play and the rules we follow feed and reinforce heterosexist myths and maintain heterosexist privilege. In many cultures, heterosexuals do not refer to themselves as such; they simply see themselves as "normal" and view people of other sexual orientations as abnormal or deviant. Cisgender heterosexual men and boys in particular, whose identification is derived largely from positioning themselves as masculine, and, therefore, as "not gay," tend to bully and degrade each other, deeming each other "sissy" or otherwise not masculine enough. Such behavior communicates that being female/feminine, transgender, or otherwise gender-nonconforming is an inferior, shameful, and less valid way of being. Moreover, the rules of a heterosexist system, which may deny same-sex couples the right to marry or to visit a partner in a hospital, reinforce the myths that heterosexuality is normal, natural, and necessary and that those who are heterosexual are more worthy of moral consideration.

Each time we play our roles and follow the rules of a nonrelational system, we further normalize and legitimize that system. But each time we refuse to do so, we help shift the system toward relational health.

5
NONRELATIONAL DISTORTIONS: PERCEPTIONS, OPPRESSION, AND INJUSTICE

All of us show bias when it comes to what information we take in. We typically focus on anything that agrees with the outcome we want.
—Noreena Hertz

IN THE CULT-CLASSIC MOVIE *The Matrix*, the characters believe themselves to be living normal lives when, in fact, they are hooked up to machines that have imprisoned their minds and the minds of almost all humans. All they see, feel, or otherwise perceive is a simulated reality, created in order to prevent them from rebelling against the machines that are using their body heat as an energy source. It's only when the characters are able to unplug themselves from the Matrix that they can free their minds and see reality as it truly is. And when they reclaim their freedom of thought, they also reclaim their freedom of choice. They no longer passively serve the violent interests of a more powerful group but instead choose to act in accordance with their personal values and integrity. They refuse to support an oppressive system, and they work for justice and freedom for all of humanity.[1]

Not unlike the Matrix, nonrelational systems coerce (and sometimes force) people into following the dictates of systems they don't even know exist, into acting against their core moral values. Most people, however, need to feel that they are living in accordance with their values, that they are living a moral life.[2] Indeed, acting against our values causes us to feel moral discomfort, a conscious or unconscious feeling of guilt, which can cause a form of cognitive dissonance.[3] In order to alleviate this dissonance, we can change our values, change our behaviors (e.g., choose not to play our roles and follow the rules when we're in a position of power), or change our perceptions of our behaviors. Most people choose the last option, and herein lies the foundation of cognitive distortions, one of the three defenses that maintain nonrelational systems.

Cognitive distortions hijack our perceptions and numb our feelings so that we engage in practices we'd otherwise likely find deeply offensive. These defenses are nonrelational ways of thinking and feeling that guide many of our behaviors. Cognitive distortions are structured to block our awareness of the consequences of our actions and to diminish our natural empathy toward others. They disconnect us from the truth of our experience, our authentic thoughts and feelings.

As noted in Chapter 4, cognitive distortions are essentially myths, all of which uphold the primary myth at the center of the nonrelational mentality: that one group (or individual) is more worthy of moral consideration than others. Each distortion acts as a distancing mechanism that disconnects us from our rationality, empathy, and ultimately, integrity.

Although cognitive distortions maintain both oppressive and abusive systems, we'll explore them primarily as they apply to oppressive systems. Oppressive systems have a more complex and entrenched defensive structure that allows for a more in-depth discussion.

The Two-Pronged Strategy of Oppressive Systems

Oppressive systems keep themselves alive by ensuring that they remain more powerful than their *countersystems*—the systems that emerge in response and as alternatives to them, that challenge them. For example, patriarchy must remain stronger than feminism, and carnism—the belief system, or ideology, that conditions people to eat certain animals and that is a subideology of speciesism—must remain stronger than veganism.[4] To this end, oppressive systems use a two-pronged defensive strategy that both strengthens the oppressive systems and weakens the countersystems.[5] This strategy causes rational, compassionate people to support irrational, harmful practices, without realizing what they are doing. And it causes them to become defensive whenever they are asked to reflect on their attitudes or behaviors, or whenever they simply observe someone following the norms of the countersystem.

This two-pronged strategy comprises two types of cognitive distortions, which are explained in detail in the next sections: *primary cognitive distortions*, which validate the oppressive system (often by validating the practice of power over), and *secondary cognitive distortions*, which invalidate the countersystem. This double strategy maintains both a power imbalance between the two opposing systems, such as that between patriarchy and feminism, and imbalance between members of opposing groups within the oppressive system itself, such as that between men and women.

Primary Cognitive Distortions

Primary cognitive distortions that are used to validate oppressive systems are based on the myth that supporting an oppressive system (e.g., maintaining white supremacy) is the right thing to do. Primary distortions legitimize the system and alter our perceptions so that we don't recognize the system's beliefs and consequences as oppressive or problematic.

Denial: See No Evil, Hear No Evil, Speak No Evil

Denial is a key distortion used by oppressive systems: if we deny there's a problem in the first place, then we don't have to do anything about it. Denial is expressed largely through the invisibility of an oppressive system. One way in which the system remains invisible is by remaining unnamed, at least before its countersystem has reached a later stage of development. (If the oppressive system has, in fact, been identified and named, we then deny that it's "as bad as it seems.") One of the roles of a countersystem is to name the oppressive system so that it may be recognized as the driver of oppression that it is and therefore be challenged. For example, if we don't name carnism, the oppressive system that veganism challenges, then eating animals appears to be simply a given, a morally neutral behavior with no basis in a belief system. We assume that only vegans and vegetarians follow a belief system, and we don't realize that when eating animals isn't a necessity—which is the case for many, though not all, people in the world today—then it is a choice, and choices always stem from beliefs. If we don't see the carnistic system for what it is, then we can neither question nor challenge it, and we don't even realize that we have a choice when it comes to eating animals.[6]

Oppressive systems also remain invisible by keeping their victims out of sight and therefore out of public consciousness. Again, the stage of development of the countersystem matters.

If the countersystem is young, then there will be less public awareness of the victimization caused by the oppressive system. To revisit the example of carnism, consider the facts that more farmed animals are killed in just one day than the total number of people killed in all wars throughout history,[7] and their body parts are literally everywhere we turn—yet we virtually never see any of these animals alive. Moreover, farmed animals endure an almost unimaginable fate: it is well documented that from birth to death, the vast majority of them[8] experience intense and unrelenting suffering.[9] Carnism depends on our denying the suffering of these individuals, because if we didn't, we would probably have a very hard time supporting their slaughter by continuing to eat them.

Ironically, as a countersystem reaches maturation, it can again struggle to expose the victimization of the oppressive system, because the violence of the oppressive system has typically become more subtle, though no less damaging. For example, in the early days of the US civil rights movement, there was extreme resistance to the idea that Black people were victimized by a racist system, even though the racism was blatant. Today, although many Americans accept that racism is a reality, there is also a narrative that the US is a "post-racial" society, making it a challenge to highlight the continued violence directed toward Black people (and toward other people who aren't white). Consider the case of Breonna Taylor, a Black woman who was killed in her home in 2020 by plainclothes officers who were executing a "no-knock" search warrant, which was partially falsified by police. At the time of this book's publication, none of the police officers involved in the raid has been convicted of a crime in relation to her killing.[10] The case is but one of an epidemic of racialized killings in the US,[11] yet the racial nature of these killings is still largely denied, masking the continued victimization of BIPOC.[12]

Of course, the central myth that denial tells is that there is no oppression in the first place, and therefore there is no unjust power imbalance.

The Three Ns of Justification:
Exercising Power Over Is Normal, Natural, and Necessary

Another cognitive distortion used by oppressive systems is justification. We are taught to justify oppressive systems, and nonrelational attitudes and behaviors in general, by believing in the three Ns of justification: that the behavior of one group exercising power over another (e.g., hetero-supremacy, male dominance, the consumption of animals) is *normal*, *natural*, and *necessary*. These are myths that are presented as facts, and they have been used to justify oppressive practices throughout the course of human history.

Exercising power over is normal

Social norms are codes of conduct, or ways of being and behaving that are considered socially acceptable and legitimate. Social norms encourage conformity: when we go along with them, our lives are easier and we're considered normal. For example, if we're cisgender and gender-conforming,[13] we'll have little to no problem finding a bathroom wherever we go, and we'll be seen as just like everybody else, as a part of the dominant group, the "normal" people. The paths of least resistance, discussed in Chapter 4, maintain the oppressive social norm; they reward conformity to the system and punish deviation from it. The social norms of an oppressive system prevent us from seeing its irrationality: when everybody's doing something, it can be difficult to see how that "something" may make very little sense. For example, many well-intentioned people support the concept of "humane" (sometimes referred to as "organic") meat. These people are willing to spend more money in order not to support animal cruelty. They are voting with their dollar, hoping to make a positive difference in the system. However, the idea of humane animal foods becomes irrational the moment we step outside the carnistic box. Most of us would consider it cruel to slaughter a happy, healthy golden retriever simply because people like the way her legs taste, yet when the very same thing is done to individuals of other species, we are told to consider it kind. Because carnism is so normal, we don't realize that "humane meat" is, in fact, a contradiction in terms.

Of course, what we call "normal" is simply the beliefs and behaviors of the dominant culture. Social norms change over time as societies evolve. For example, it was once widely acceptable to stone women who were suspected of infidelity[14] (it still is in a few places), or to refer to people in wheelchairs and people with other kinds of disabilities as "invalids"[15] and construct environments that made it impossible for them to participate in social life.[16] These behaviors are now considered reprehensible, at least in many places in the world.

Cultural relativism is another way oppressive dynamics may be seen as normal and therefore justifiable. Cultural relativism is the belief that the values and practices of a culture should not be judged as unethical simply based on how they compare to those of other cultures. In this view, North Americans, for example, shouldn't deem eating dogs unethical when it is a cultural norm in other cultures.

Although it's important to consider and respect differences in cultural norms as we work to end oppression, it's also important to recognize that cultural relativism can be used as a justification for oppression. For example, although we would obviously not want to promote racist or ethnocentric attitudes by judging people who eat dogs, at the same time, we would not want to conclude that because people eat dogs in some places this means that consuming animals is a morally neutral behavior. Many, perhaps most, oppressive systems are global, so just because one culture may have a different way of expressing and sustaining the system does not mean that the behavior is not oppressive. In short, Asian carnism does not justify North American carnism any more than African heterosexism justifies European heterosexism. Even though the *content* of an oppressive system may change—dogs rather than cows may be consumed, for example—the *process* of exercising power over others, the process of oppression, remains the same.

Exercising power over is natural

Oppressive systems also justify themselves by presenting their tenets as natural, or "the way things are meant to be." This myth is maintained in large part by the disciplines of science and history.

When we look at science through the lens of an oppressive system, we construct research that confirms the belief that one group is naturally superior to (and therefore more worthy of moral consideration than) another, and in so doing, we legitimize unjust power imbalances and oppression. Consider the Nazis' use of craniometry and eugenics, or what feminist researcher Cordelia Fine refers to as "neurosexist" research—pseudoneuroscience that is used to demonstrate that, for example, females are biologically better at empathizing with (and therefore caregiving for) others.[17]

When we look at history through the lens of an oppressive system, what we seek and how we interpret what we discover legitimize the system. For example, when the Nazis looked at history through the lens of anti-Semitism, they sought—and found—evidence "proving" the "natural" inferiority of Jewish people. Indeed, what we learn to call "natural" is often simply the dominant culture's interpretation of history.

Exercising power over is necessary

Justifying oppressive behaviors as necessary is perhaps the most powerful way to sustain an oppressive system. If we believe that a practice is a necessity—for the maintenance of the social order, the survival of a race or species, and so on—then it becomes inevitable and, as such, exempt from ethical examination. The behavior is seen as a given rather than as a choice. For example, if we believe that keeping our national borders closed to refugees or invading other countries that host potential threats to our own country are necessary for our security, then those measures seem like merely a matter of self-defense: if we don't kill others, we will die (or be harmed) ourselves. Most genocidal propaganda has relied on promoting the practice of power over as necessary. In this way they garner the widespread approval of people whose fear drives them to support practices that are deeply opposed to their core moral values. Consider, for instance, how the Rwandan ruling party, which was dominated by Hutus, claimed that total extermination of the Tutsi opposition, which included all Tutsi "accomplices" (i.e., civilians), was an act of self-defense.[18] Or consider Nazi minister of propaganda Joseph Goebbels's claim that Bolsheviks and Jews were one and the same and that "Bolshevism [was] the declaration of war by Jewish-led international subhumans against culture itself."[19] One of the key aims of justice movements is to debunk the myth of necessity, because as soon as a behavior is recognized as a choice rather than a given, it takes on an ethical dimension it didn't previously have.

Often, what we learn to think of as necessary is simply what's necessary to maintain an oppressive system. For example, to preserve a system that privileges the very wealthy, it is indeed necessary to continue capitalist financial policies that make it difficult or impossible for those from working-class communities or communities of people experiencing poverty to access the education, training, and networks they need in order to be truly upwardly mobile.

Institutionalized Oppression

Oppressive systems are institutionalized, meaning that they are supported and promoted by all major social institutions, such as medicine, law, education, and business. In other words, these systems are woven into the structure of society, shaping norms, laws, traditions, and our very way of life. When a system is institutionalized, its beliefs and practices are promoted as facts rather than opinions and are accepted unquestioningly by the majority. For example, a strong bias against homosexuality was once institutionalized (and still is, in some places in the world). Homosexuality was classified by the medical community as a mental illness; same-sex couples were not allowed to marry; and heterosexuality was considered the normal, natural, and necessary way of life for all people.

When we are born into an institutionalized system, we absorb the system's logic as our own. In other words, we internalize it.

Internalized Oppression

Oppressive systems use a set of cognitive distortions designed to *other* their victims, causing us (when we're in a powerholding position) to perceive them as fundamentally different from and inferior to ourselves—as separate from us and less worthy than we are. These distortions are *objectification*, *deindividualization*, and *dichotomization*.

Objectification—perceiving someone as an object—can be seen in how patriarchy teaches us to view girls and women as sexual playthings for men's gratification or how ableism leads us to view people with disabilities as objects of inspiration to motivate us. So, for instance, men may refer to a woman as a "piece of ass," and nondisabled people may seek to get a warm, fuzzy feeling from watching "inspiration porn," sensationalized depictions of people with disabilities purportedly overcoming adversity.[20] Deindividualization—perceiving someone as an abstraction that lacks individuality or a personality—can be seen in how ableist culture instills in us the view that people who have disabilities are all alike: they are all lumped together, referred to as "disabled." So we are encouraged to assume, for example, that a person who is blind but can walk shares the same experience as a person who is sighted but is in a wheelchair. And dichotomization—placing individuals into oppositional categories in our minds so that we harbor different feelings and carry out different behaviors toward members of different groups—is exemplified by the belief that Muslims are dangerous and Christians are trustworthy, or that working-class teenagers or teenagers experiencing poverty who are smoking pot are "slackers," whereas wealthy teens doing the same are "experimenting" or "being kids."

Secondary Cognitive Distortions: Invalidating Countersystems

When enough people start to question and then challenge an oppressive system, a countersystem is formed, which may evolve into a justice movement. Of course, as closed systems that resist change, oppressive systems fight back. When we look back on history, we can see that many of the beliefs that we today accept as rational, ethical, and essential to a functional society were at one point or another dismissed, invalidated, ridiculed, and even met with violent hostility. For example, it was once considered ludicrous and offensive for BIPOC to patronize the same institutions as did white people or for women to attend university, and those who challenged such norms were socially ostracized and sometimes even imprisoned or killed.

A backlash is the reaction of an oppressive system to its power being threatened; it is an attempt to regain lost power. An oppressive system, which is based on a mythology, creates new myths, and sometimes strengthens existing ones, to prevent us from taking seriously any challenges to the system. Such myths seek to invalidate the countersystem and those who represent it. For example, as feminists have challenged the misogynistic attitudes that drive traditional, or hostile sexism, *benevolent sexism*—which idealizes rather than disparages women, but which nevertheless maintains gender bias and therefore patriarchy—has emerged as a more modern and insidious form of sexism.

Despite the fact that most people's values and interests are in alignment with countersystems, most people are also resistant to hearing the truth about oppressive systems. This is because an oppressive system causes people to reject the very information that would free them, psychologically and emotionally, from the system's coercive influence. It does this by using secondary cognitive distortions, which are myths that seek to invalidate the countersystem and those who represent it.

Secondary distortions invalidate three aspects of a counter-system: its justice movement, its ideology, and its proponents or advocates.[21]

Secondary distortions, like primary distortions, are internalized, shaping our perceptions without our realizing it. They shape the perceptions of the powerholders within an oppressive system and, often, those of the proponents of the countersystem. For example, both men and women alike may believe the myth that women are overly emotional. So boys and men see girls and women as less able to be objective, and girls and women, including many feminists, doubt their ability to be rational and feel ashamed of their own emotional reactions. When proponents of a countersystem have internalized the myths of secondary distortions, they can end up feeling confused, frustrated, and despairing, which limits their ability to effectively promote their cause.

Secondary Denial:
Invalidating Counterideologies and Justice Movements

Secondary denial teaches us to deny the fact that the countersystem is a valid belief system or, in the case of young movements such as the vegan movement, that it represents a valid justice movement. We learn, for example, to believe that veganism is simply a "trend," so we fail to recognize that the vegan movement is based on the very same principles as are other justice movements, principles such as promoting compassion and justice and challenging the notion that a group with more power (humans) should have the right to enact violence against a group with less power (nonhuman animals) to serve the former's own ends (i.e., producing and consuming carnistic products).

Moreover, whereas primary denial teaches us to believe that there is no oppressive system in the first place, secondary denial teaches us to believe that, therefore, there is no power imbalance between the dominant group and the nondominant group. So we assume that the playing field is level when it comes to interactions and relationships between members of these groups, and we fail to see how the re-creation of nonrelational dynamics in our daily lives helps keep oppressive systems in place. For example, studies have shown that in mixed-gender interactions, men are more likely to interrupt women,[22] to speak for and about them,[23] and to condescendingly explain things to them ("mansplaining").[24] All of these conversational dynamics mirror and bolster the patriarchal myths that men are more authoritative and are meant to be dominant. But because we have learned to deny that there's a power imbalance between men and women, when a cisgender heterosexual couple enacts such a dynamic, it's rarely noticed. If it is noticed, it's typically assumed to reflect individual personality differences rather than a gendered imbalance of power that derives from and maintains an oppressive system.

Professionals, too, may unwittingly sustain oppressive systems when they buy into the myths of secondary denial (and other distortions). For example, despite a plethora of literature documenting that in heterosexual romantic partnerships, women are more likely to be victims of abuse than men,[25] and despite decades of feminist research unearthing the significant power imbalance between male and female domestic partners, many psychotherapists still counsel heterosexual couples as though the partners bring equal levels of power to the table, and they also fail to recognize domestic abuse (which is epidemic in the US and many other places in the world) when it is happening.[26] Domestic violence expert Lundy Bancroft points out how countless therapists will, for example, suggest that an abusive man has an "anger management problem," or that he's just reacting to his partner "pushing his buttons" or "reminding him of his mother," rather than recognize and address the underlying problem of unbalanced power roles and male entitlement.[27]

Projection: Shooting the Messenger

Perhaps the most common secondary distortion used by oppressive systems is projection—ascribing to proponents or advocates of countersystems negative and inaccurate ideas that invalidate their message. Projection is a form of shooting the messenger: if we shoot the messenger, we don't have to take seriously the implications of their message.[28]

Projection is often expressed through the negative stereotyping of advocates of countersystems. When people believe in these stereotypes, they are not only more resistant to the information being shared by those advocates but also less likely to feel connected to the advocates themselves, even those with whom they may be in close relationship. Stereotypes reduce people to one-dimensional caricatures and focus on the negative, making it difficult for us to relate to those being stereotyped. Stereotypes also cause us to assume that all people in the stereotyped group are alike—that, for example, all lesbians are the same. We may then use one negative encounter with a lesbian LGBTQ+ advocate as an excuse to invalidate the message of all LGBTQ+ advocates. Ultimately, negative stereotypes of advocates cause us to see ourselves as being in opposition to those we might otherwise consider natural allies.

Many advocates are stereotyped as "overly emotional," a framing that easily discredits their message. Overly emotional people are, by definition, not rational, and irrational people are not worth listening to. Perhaps not surprisingly, this stereotype has been used throughout human history to discredit those challenging oppressive systems: the abolitionists working to end slavery in the US were called "sentimentalists,"[29] and the suffragists who championed women's right to vote were portrayed as "hysterical."[30] And consider how the contemporary popular media frames anti-racism protests: Black and Brown protesters are often referred to as "thugs" who are "rioting," whereas white people engaging in the very same behaviors but with less noble motivations, flooding the streets and shouting after their sports team won a match, are referred to as "fans" who are "celebrating."[31]

Sometimes, those who oppose an oppressive system are stereotyped as being against members of the public who represent the establishment being challenged. For example, feminists are portrayed as "anti-male" (even though feminism ultimately seeks to free people of all genders, including men and boys, from the violent, dysfunctional, and nonrelational limitations patriarchy imposes on them). And LGBTQ+ advocates are often framed as "anti-family." This "anti" stereotype is based largely on the assumption that people can't be, for example, pro-female *and* pro-male, supportive of LGBTQ+ relationships *and* supportive of cisgender heterosexual couples. In fact, the opposite is more likely to be the case: compassion begets compassion. The more compassion we allow into our lives, the more compassion we are likely to feel overall. Framing advocates as "anti" is an effective way to reduce their threat to the oppressive system. If much of the population believes that advocates are against it, then the countermovement will not attract enough supporters to weaken the oppressive system it's challenging.

Another projection is that of the "omniscient" advocate, expressed through the expectation that every advocate should have a fully conceptualized system ready to be put in place to replace the one they are opposing, which, of course, is impossible. For example, those who challenge capitalism or environmental exploitation may be expected to have all the answers to the problems of the system they're criticizing—to be experts on economics, politics, philosophy, ecology, agriculture, and so on.[32] And when they can't answer all the questions thrown their way, or even when they can but their responses aren't considered legitimate, their entire ideology may come into question. The implication is that someone has the right to challenge an oppressive system only when they have all the solutions to the problems caused by it.

In addition, advocates may be expected to live up to an impossible ideal. For example, women are expected to climb to the top of the professional ladder, but they may find that they have to act like men in order to do so, because "masculine" qualities, such as stoicism and assertiveness, are necessary for success in many professions. When they act like men, however, they are criticized for being "cold" or "bitchy." Yet if they decide to act like women, they are stereotyped as shallow and vain or too weak for the job.[33]

Sometimes, advocates are stereotyped as mentally ill. Pathologizing those who challenge oppressive systems isn't new: before the abolition of slavery in the US, for example, people classified as slaves who attempted to escape were diagnosed with the mental illness "drapetomania," as it was considered crazy not to want to be enslaved.[34]

Secondary Justification

Whereas primary justification teaches us to believe that the tenets of the oppressive systems are normal, natural, and necessary, secondary justification teaches us to believe that the tenets of the countersystem are *ab*normal, *un*natural, and *un*necessary. Consider how this framing has been used, for example, to invalidate the LGBTQ+ movement by invalidating those representing it: until 1973, homosexuality was classified as a mental illness in the *Diagnostic and Statistical Manual of Mental Disorders II*, the bible of US psychiatry.[35] Although public opinion has changed significantly since then, similar anti-LGBTQ+ rhetoric nevertheless persists. Secondary justification has also been used to invalidate feminism by perpetuating the myth that girls and women being granted equal social power and control is abnormal, unnatural, and unnecessary. As a result, girls and women tend to automatically cede power and control to boys and men, and the patriarchal power imbalance is maintained.

Decreasing the Power of Distortions through Increasing Awareness

Social transformation is not about simply eliminating a particular behavior; it is about transforming the system that gives rise to that behavior in the first place. Of course, systems and the behaviors they breed are part of a feedback loop: the more we engage in the behavior, the more we reinforce the mythology of the system, and vice versa. So, social change relies on our ability to both provide incentives for behavioral change (by making it easier to make more environmentally friendly lifestyle choices, for example) and expose the defenses that keep oppressive systems alive (by raising awareness of the defensive structure of oppressive systems and debunking the myths they are based on).

Transforming an oppressive system therefore requires developing an awareness of the elusive nature of its distortions. These defenses attempt to invalidate anything—any idea, person, behavior, and so on—that challenges the system. Even some of the most rational and progressive individuals can end up defending an oppressive system whose structure they are unaware of. For example, during the American Civil War, some moderates argued that although slavery was wrong, enslaved people were not actually capable of taking care of themselves, so it was ultimately better for them to remain enslaved.[36] Often, logical fallacies are the result not of an inability to think logically but of the distorted thinking that emerges when an oppressive system is seeking to defend itself.

Indeed, research suggests that when people become aware of their cognitive distortions, they are less influenced by them,[37] so it stands to reason that such awareness can weaken oppressive systems. In other words, when people become aware of not only the consequences of an oppressive system—such as the extensive nonhuman animal suffering and environmental degradation that result from carnism[38]—but also of the cognitive distortions of the system, they may be better able to make choices that reflect their authentic thoughts and feelings, rather than what they've been conditioned to think and feel. Only with awareness can people make their choices freely, because without awareness, there *is* no free choice.

6
NONRELATIONAL NARRATIVES: THE STORIES OF INJUSTICE

What happens is of little significance compared with
the stories we tell ourselves about what happens.
—Rabbih Alameddine

IN 2008, AN ADVERTISING INTERN inadvertently came up with what turned out to be an ingenious idea for a marketing campaign for the breakfast cereal Shreddies.[1] Shreddies were little whole-wheat squares, similar to Chex, and the campaign sought to increase the appeal (and therefore the sales) of the cereal without changing a single aspect of the product itself. The strategy? To transform public perception such that the commonplace squares became special diamonds. So Shreddies were reborn as Diamond Shreddies, and they boasted a market share increase of 18 percent during the first month of what became an award-winning campaign.

The Diamond Shreddies campaign offers a poignant example of the power of storytelling. When we look back over the course of history, we can see that it is shaped by many factors, perhaps the most powerful of which is stories. Beneath every oppressive system and every countersystem that seeks to challenge it are stories that guide one or the other. We cannot, for example, take up arms against others without first believing the story that those others are enemies who must be conquered. And we cannot stand together in protest against a violent invasion without believing the story that the invasion is unjust. Stories shape our world and our lives, for better or worse. So understanding the stories of oppressive systems and how they influence our perceptions and guide our behaviors is vital to transforming oppression.

Narratives

Our narrative is the story we create based on our beliefs and perceptions. Narratives can emerge from our personal experience or from the social conditioning we inherited from society. For example, if someone has a personal history of being betrayed in relationships, they may have developed a narrative that people cannot be trusted. And if someone grows up in a heterosexist society, their inherited narrative may be that heterosexuality is normal and natural and that other sexual orientations are abnormal and unnatural. Often, our narratives are a synthesis of our personal experience and social experience.[2]

Narratives shape our perceptions, which give rise to our feelings. Together, our perceptions and feelings drive our behaviors. For example, if your partner left the kitchen in a mess before leaving for work in the morning and your narrative is that they just didn't care enough to pick up after themself, you may feel angry and therefore criticize them when you see them later. However, if your narrative were instead that they were in a rush and ran out of time, you would feel and respond differently. On a larger scale, when the widely accepted narrative was that women were too irrational to make sound and objective decisions, people feared and distrusted women's ability to manage power and so denied them the right to vote.[3]

Dominant, nonrelational narratives (which I'll be referring to as either "dominant narratives" or "nonrelational narratives" to avoid cumbersome wording—with the understanding that not all dominant narratives are nonrelational but those to which I refer in this chapter are) are the narratives of the individual or group with more power in a nonrelational system. Although a dominant narrative sometimes reflects a cognitive distortion, such as the myth that "Christian supremacy is normal," dominant narratives are often made up of several such myths, woven together to create an elaborate fiction that's far more difficult to debunk than a single falsehood. Dominant narratives are like perceptual tapestries, which are greater than the sum of their parts and are much more challenging to unravel than an individual tangled string of yarn. These nonrelational narratives mirror and bolster the mythology of the nonrelational system, and members of all groups—dominant and nondominant—grow up learning and often believing them.[4] For example, both heterosexuals and non-heterosexuals learn to believe the heterosexist narrative that heterosexuality is normal and natural and that other sexualities are abnormal and unnatural, or deviant, which is one reason for the high rates of suicide among LGBTQ+ teenagers.[5] Nonrelational narratives are constructed to delude people into supporting oppression and to silence the voices of people who seek to tell the truth.

Dominant narratives are perhaps the most powerful defense sustaining nonrelational systems, and they are also the most difficult to challenge: they coerce us into doing their bidding while preventing us from seeing the consequences of our actions and making us believe that we are operating of our own free will. These narratives are like living entities that take up residence in our psyches without our awareness, with a survival instinct that drives them to keep themselves alive. Unbeknownst to us, we look at the world through the eyes of a narrative that feeds on whatever validates it and rejects anything that might alert us to the fact that we've been psychologically possessed.[6]

Unbalanced Trust Narratives

Nonrelational systems maintain or grow their unjust power imbalances in large part by conditioning us to have a skewed sense of trust in the narratives of opposing groups within these systems. We learn to trust dominant narratives too much and the challenging narratives, or *counternarratives*, too little. Our unbalanced trust in narratives is, perhaps above all else, what keeps nonrelational systems intact. Whether on the broadest societal level or the most intimate interpersonal level, our tendency to trust narratives either too much or too little is the lifeblood of these systems.

In a nonrelational system, those with less power are more likely to see themselves through the eyes of those with more power, and to believe the latter's narrative, than vice versa. Whenever there's a power differential, this is the case: consider, for example, how much more impact the insult "you're stupid" has when said by a parent to a child than the other way around. This is one reason why the very people who would normally oppose an oppressive system can end up supporting it. For example, LGBTQ+ teenagers living in a heterosexist, genderist social system often believe that something is wrong with them, even when their own narrative and associated feelings are perfectly natural for them. Likewise, many girls and women believe that their primary value comes from being physically attractive to boys and men, even though they know, on some level, that their value goes much deeper. Moreover, studies have found that older people tend to perceive themselves as—

and therefore to act—less physically and sexually vital than they actually are, having bought into the narratives of an ageist system.[7]

Defining Reality:
The Mass Hypnosis of Nonrelational Systems

Defining reality is dictating the truth of another's experience—appointing oneself the expert on what another is thinking or feeling, even when they say otherwise.[8] For example, a boy falls and scrapes his knee and starts crying, only to be told that the cut "isn't that bad" and therefore that "there's no reason to be upset." The boy learns to distrust the signals his body and feelings are giving him, and as similar experiences build up over the years, he grows into a man who has to be on his deathbed before he'll see a doctor and who finds it nearly impossible to identify and articulate his emotions. On the societal level, we see the same phenomenon play out as the dominant white culture continues to assert that racism no longer exists, despite repeated commentary from BIPOC whose personal experiences directly contradict that claim.[9] On the intrapersonal level, we can define our own reality—saying to ourselves, for example, that we "shouldn't" be feeling depressed because what we're experiencing "isn't such a big deal." (Note that when we define our reality, we are judging ourselves and framing our experience as "wrong." This is not the same as objectively reflecting on our experience and, for instance, considering whether we may be catastrophizing.)

Defining reality is problematic no matter who does it or why it is done, because the process is fundamentally invalidating. This act communicates that another's experience and, by extension, their self are invalid. To be invalid is to be wrong or to be worthless. So defining reality is shaming. It is also disempowering and disconnecting—that is, it's fundamentally nonrelational.

Defining reality is the foundation of psychological abuse, and it is an essential weapon in the arsenal of cult leaders, domestic abusers, totalitarian rulers, and anyone who seeks power and control over others. It causes others to lose trust in their thoughts and feelings, eroding their self-confidence and stripping them of their sense of empowerment and agency. In its extreme form, defining reality is "gaslighting"—intentionally getting another or others to distrust their experience such that they lose the ability to know what's real, therefore turning all power and control over to the gaslighter. Consider, for example, how Donald Trump is known for repeatedly stating that the news media—meant to act as the eyes and ears of the public—is not to be trusted,[10] and how public trust in the media plummeted as a result.[11]

When a totalitarian leader succeeds, completely or even only partially, in defining reality, the consequences can be catastrophic. When Vladimir Putin first invaded Ukraine in 2014 to annex Crimea, a major pillar of his propaganda was that the West had crossed a "red line" by backing the new government in Kyiv. By the second invasion in the spring of 2022, that narrative of justification had been perpetuated and expanded to include the claim that NATO was actively planning to attack Russia, and that Russia and the Russian way of life were at serious risk of being dominated and suppressed. As such, Putin secured the backing of much of the Russian public, as well as that of key allies, such as the Chinese government.

The more a powerholder defines another's reality, the more the other believes the powerholder's version of reality over their own, and therefore the more they shape their life to appease the needs and wants of the powerholder. For example, in an abusive relationship, the person being abused often ends up making excuses for the abuser's behavior ("He's just going through a stressful period," or "I'm not that easy to live with either"). The abused person typically assumes responsibility for the abuse ("I shouldn't have been so critical; then she wouldn't have gotten so mad at me"), overfocuses on the needs of the abuser, and neglects themself so that their perceptions and world revolve around the abuser. Often, the abuser isolates the person being abused, cutting them off from outside voices that would challenge the abuser's version of reality. A similar dynamic can be seen on the societal level, between a powerholding group and a non-powerholding group. For example, the lack of accurate representations of Asian Americans in popular US culture reinforces shallow stereotypes of members of this group—that of the high-achieving math student, the martial artist, or the sexualized geisha—while the overrepresentation of white people reinforces whiteness as the norm and the cultural ideal. This narrative defines the reality of Asian Americans such that they often end up conforming to the white norm and adapting in order to meet the needs of white people, who occupy most positions of power and are the primary cultural decision-makers.

Whenever we impose our narrative on others, we are defining their reality—and dominant, nonrelational narratives are imposed on everyone, creating a sort of mass hypnosis. These narratives are woven into our world and our lives to create a web of myths in which we're all ensnared but which virtually none of us can see.

When Narratives Clash

Confirmation bias is the tendency for people to seek, notice, and remember only information that supports their existing assumptions—that confirms their narrative.[12] If, for example, we believe that humans are fundamentally good, we'll tend to notice all the examples of how helpful and kind people are and to overlook, explain away, or forget evidence that disproves this belief. And if we live in a culture that shares our narrative, our cognitive biases will be that much stronger. The more people there are who support a narrative, the more entrenched it becomes.

Because of the near-universal acceptance of dominant narratives as truths rather than beliefs and therefore as facts rather than opinions, the confirmation bias in favor of dominant narratives and the inaccuracies that inevitably result from this bias remain invisible. For this reason, dominant narratives aren't held to the same standards of accountability as are counternarratives. When nearly everyone agrees on something, they are unlikely to feel the need to examine it to ensure that it's actually accurate. For example, because just about everyone in the medical community in the fourteenth century believed in alchemy, which is the practice of transmuting metals to treat disease, alchemists were not held accountable for their methodology: they were not expected to prove that it was sound. And when alchemy did begin to come under scrutiny, the burden of proof lay with those representing the nondominant method, chemistry.[13]

In a nonrelational system, when dominant and nondominant narratives clash or compete, the dominant narrative, which is less accountable, is nevertheless more believable to the majority. For example, when BIPOC describe their experiences of racism, white people often argue that such commentary is a distortion or exaggeration of the facts, and the dominant white narrative is more readily believed. But given that the oppressive system of racism is so deeply entrenched that it impacts virtually all racial interactions—whether we are aware of this fact or not—and given that the dominant white narrative (and white privilege, an issue we'll discuss in the following chapter) prevents white people from recognizing the experiences of BIPOC and causes them to define the reality of BIPOC, it is far more likely that a BIPOC's account of their experience of racism is accurate and a white person's perceptions are not.

Furthermore, because those with less power tend to distrust their own narratives and to (consciously or unconsciously) believe those of the dominant group (or individual), they tend to feel less confident and perhaps even intimidated when narratives clash, which often prevents them from speaking out. So when a member of a nondominant group does challenge a dominant narrative, chances are they have more than ample reason to do so.

The Nonrelational Metanarrative

The *metanarrative*, or overarching narrative, underlying all nonrelational systems is that there is a hierarchy of moral worth, that certain groups are more worthy of moral consideration than others. Specific subnarratives reinforce this metanarrative, largely by communicating that the experiences, thoughts and opinions, feelings, and needs of powerholders are more valid than those of others. For example, when white Europeans express their anger about African and Asian immigrants "taking their jobs," the rest of society is expected to feel more concerned about the former's experience—to empathize more with them—than about that of the immigrants, who, as residents or citizens, are equally entitled to those jobs.

Because nonrelational narratives are invalidating, they are typically shaming. As we discussed previously, shaming members of nondominant groups serves to maintain oppressive systems. People who feel ashamed lack the confidence and motivation to recognize and challenge an unfair system, to take positive action on their own or sometimes others' behalf. (Of course, shaming those with less power helps maintain all nonrelational systems, oppressive and abusive.)

There are countless nonrelational narratives that impact the perceptions of members of both dominant and nondominant groups. Most notable are those narratives that cause us to perceive members of nondominant groups as deficient and members of dominant groups as more authoritative; that distort our perceptions of needs, control, and anger; and that reinforce prejudicial attitudes toward members of nondominant groups.

Narratives and Deficiency

Dominant narratives often depict members of nondominant groups as deficient.[14] Because dominant groups represent the standard for everyone and are held up as the ideal, members of nondominant groups are, by comparison, perceived as less-than— less attractive than, less competent than, less "cultured" than, and so forth. For example, in ableist culture, individuals are labeled "disabled" when their ability to participate in one or more central life activities, such as social interaction or ambulation, is impaired. Not only does the term "disabled" frame individuals dealing with these kinds of issues as deficient, since it focuses on the fact that they are *not* able to do something—that they are lacking an ability—but it can also end up defining their identity in the eyes of others (and of themselves, if they're not aware of the influence of the ableist narrative). The "disability" can become a central feature of how they are perceived. Moreover, the very concept of "disabled" reflects an arbitrary categorization. We ascribe this label to, for example, an emotionally intelligent individual who is missing an arm, but not to someone who is self-centered and exploitative but who has both arms intact. Which of these individuals needs more special treatment and accommodation? For which of them must other individuals and society pay a higher price?[15]

Narratives, Needs, and Perceptions of Control

Although a variety of factors, such as our temperament and personal history, affect how we relate to our own and others' needs, nonrelational narratives play an important role. Nonrelational systems teach us to view our needs as being too important when we have more power than another, or as not important enough when we have less power than another. When we view our needs as overly important, we feel a sense of entitlement. Entitlement is having a double standard, believing that we are deserving of special treatment. The rules that we expect others to follow don't apply to us. For example, a domestic abuser may expect his partner to listen and respond to him when he's upset about something she did, but when she asks for the same, he feels unfairly put upon and feels angry, as anger is the emotional response to (perceived or actual) injustice. Similarly, although in some parts of the US the population of native Spanish speakers outnumbers that of native English speakers, many native English speakers feel resentful for having to view public signs that are bilingual.[16]

When we have an overblown sense of the importance of our needs, we also tend to view others' requests to have their needs met not as neutral requests but as unfair demands. We can therefore feel controlled—even when we're not—and react accordingly. So members of dominant groups may become righteously angry when their needs aren't met, and they can feel defensive when asked to meet the needs of members of nondominant groups. For example, research has shown that among married couples, even when both spouses work full time, women do 70–80 percent of the domestic work, including childcare. And when women ask for a more equitable division of labor, men perceive such requests as unfair demands.[17] Indeed, popular culture frequently portrays women as though they "don't mind" scrubbing dirty toilets or changing soiled diapers as much as men do, as though women somehow have a higher tolerance for the discomfort of domestic drudgery.

Moreover, because members of nondominant groups have learned to devalue and dismiss their own needs, they can have trouble even recognizing these needs. If, for example, a woman believes that her male partner's need to feel free and uncontrolled is more important than her need to feel secure and respected, she may tell herself she's just overreacting when he does things such as flirting with other people. In addition, even if a member of a nondominant group does recognize a need of their own, they may have trouble articulating it because they sense that the powerholder may respond with anger and because they believe in the narrative that they're making unfair demands. If they do articulate this need, they can end up feeling guilty and ashamed, believing that what they're asking for is invalid and unjust. Consider, for instance, how ensuring that a person with a disability is able to simply function (e.g., providing tactile flooring) is typically seen as an "accommodation" and an inconvenience rather than as a matter of honoring a basic human right.

When requests based on the needs of members of nondominant groups are seen as controlling demands, even seemingly benign needs that have no bearing or impact on the needs of members of dominant groups can be perceived as impositions. Because of the carnistic narrative, for example, vegan parents who raise their children accordingly are often accused of "imposing their veganism on their children," whereas nonvegan parents are never seen as "imposing their carnism on their children." The oppressive system of carnism also prevents us from appreciating the fact that parents naturally raise their children according to their own beliefs, which is why we don't expect Christians to raise their children as atheists or Democrats to raise their children as Republicans. (I am referring to vegans as members of a nondominant ideological group who, because of this status, are sometimes on the lower end of a power differential. I do not mean to suggest that vegans as a group have the same kind of experience as do, for instance, BIPOC or Jewish people.)

Narratives and Authority

A central tenet of nonrelational systems is *authoritarianism*—the belief that power should be concentrated in the hands of those deemed appropriate to exercise authority over others, and that such authority is more valuable than personal freedom. Of course, this tenet is typically not explicitly stated. Sometimes, it's even ostensibly opposed by an oppressive system, as in the case of capitalism, a system that claims to support democratization and decentralization of power, even as it centralizes power.[18] To maintain themselves, nonrelational systems need to promote authoritarianism. People who have been conditioned to trust powerholders' opinions over their own are more likely to defer to the powerholders' objectives of maintaining nonrelational systems and are less likely to question or challenge those systems.

These *authoritarian narratives* cause us to believe that the opinions of members of dominant groups hold more weight than do those of members of nondominant groups—and if there is a difference of opinion, to place the burden of proof on the latter. Indeed, powerholders tend to see themselves as more informed than they actually are. They also tend to perceive their opinions as facts and the facts shared by members of nondominant groups as opinions. This is partly why potentially productive conversations about oppression end up as destructive debates. Opinions are subjective and open to debate, whereas facts are objective and therefore not disputable. For example, a gender-nonconforming person is generally much more informed about issues of gender than is the average cisgender heterosexual person. Yet if the topic of gender arises in a conversation between members of these different groups, the cisgender heterosexual person may argue passionately about issues they don't actually understand and insist that the gender-nonconforming person is wrong about the main ideas and practices of their own lifestyle. The cisgender heterosexual person believes that the gender-nonconforming person should have to prove the validity of their position, while resisting the facts that person is sharing.

Moreover, studies have shown that when people are in positions of power, they actually feel less empathy for others and are more likely to rely on stereotypes and generalizations when making judgments about others.[19] So they tend to be less open to narratives that challenge their authority. This mentality, of course, helps to maintain authoritarian narratives.

Narratives and Anger

Nonrelational narratives distort perceptions of anger. Because anger—which is the emotion that arises as a reaction to unjust attitudes and behaviors—drives people to challenge injustice, it is a threat to systems that are based on injustice. If enough people within an oppressive system are in touch with and able to express their anger about it, the system becomes destabilized. When someone who challenges the system expresses anger, their anger is often perceived as more intense than it actually is. Furthermore, they are often framed as "an angry person" rather than as "a person who is angry." The focus is on a supposed internal problem with the individual rather than on the external circumstances about which they are angry. For example, when women discuss sexism, the slightest hint of anger is often seen as aggression and the women are labeled "bitches" or worse, making their anger seem like a problematic aspect of their character rather than a legitimate emotional response to the injustice of patriarchy.[20] And the all-too-common stereotype of the "angry Black woman" demonstrates how this problem is compounded by race.

Narratives and Prejudice

Nonrelational systems rely on narratives that reflect and bolster prejudice. As countersystems evolve, the narratives of oppressive systems are identified and challenged and the prejudice becomes more visible. For example, although anti-Semitism is still very much a problem today and is even on the rise in certain places in the world,[21] in at least some places, this prejudice has been named and challenged such that mocking a Jewish person for not eating pork is no longer tolerated in many circles. But when a countersystem is young, nonrelational narratives can remain hidden and wreak havoc. For instance, because veganism is still an emerging countersystem, the ideological minority status of vegans is largely unrecognized, and prejudice against vegans is almost entirely invisible. Hostile humor directed toward members of this group, often in public—mocking them for not eating animals and attacking their values and character—is commonplace and considered socially acceptable, as it is not yet recognized as the prejudicial behavior it is.

Internalized Oppression and Internalized Privilege

Internalized oppression is the phenomenon whereby those with less power in an oppressive (or abusive) system believe in their inferiority and act in ways that mirror and reinforce this belief. Often, this means they have bought into the negative narratives they've heard about themselves.[22] Internalized oppression causes individuals and groups to act against their own interests by participating in their own oppression and in the oppression of others within their group.

For example, many women internalize the sexist narrative that their primary value comes from being sexually attractive to men, and they end up competing with one another for men's attention rather than uniting to transform the oppressive system of patriarchy that causes them to believe they are only as worthy as they are (heterosexually) attractive.

The flip side of internalized oppression is *internalized privilege.* Internalized privilege is the phenomenon whereby dominant groups or individuals in a nonrelational system believe in their superiority and as such feel entitled to special treatment that is withheld from others, and they act accordingly. Internalized oppression and privilege create a narrative cocktail that can act as a social narcotic, inebriating us so that we continue to play our roles in and follow the rules of nonrelational systems without realizing what we're doing. (The next chapter explores the concept of privilege more fully.)

Oppressive Systems and the Trauma Narrative

Atrocities are the inevitable end result of unchecked nonrelational behaviors, the ultimate expression of oppressive systems. Even if the violence of an oppressive system is manifested as "only" discriminatory and unfair treatment in one part of the world, elsewhere, the system may be genocidal. For example, anti-Semitism was (and is) a global system of oppression that found its genocidal expression in Nazi Germany.

Atrocities are mass traumatic phenomena, and as such, they often cause both victims and witnesses to become traumatized. The victims of atrocities range from children and their parents who were separated at the US–Mexican border to Muslims whose communities were bombed by invaders. The witnesses are often those who are active in countersystems, who may or may not have been victimized by oppressive systems. As advocates for the victims, the witnesses are proponents of social causes or justice movements designed to end the violence of oppressive systems—people such as doctors on humanitarian missions in war zones, social workers who run shelters for domestic abuse survivors, and vegan advocates who capture and share graphic imagery of violence against nonhuman animals.

People who have been exposed to an atrocity can develop a worldview that's based on trauma, or a *trauma narrative*, in which they see the world as one ongoing traumatic event with only three roles to be played—victim, perpetrator, and hero. The more traumatized the person becomes, the more rigidly they may compartmentalize these roles, with little room left for nuance. Advocates who fight among themselves are sometimes acting out the trauma narrative. Unable to accept that good people participate in harmful practices, they assume that if someone is not acting perfectly in accordance with the ideology of the countersystem, then that person is a perpetrator. In other words, if someone is not a victim, then they're either a perpetrator or a hero, and heroes must be all good, all the time.

The trauma narrative is often part of a post-traumatic stress syndrome, in which thoughts, emotions, and physical experiences become distorted and unbalanced. People who suffer from post-traumatic stress and are looking at the world through the lens of the trauma narrative can end up exacerbating their own traumatization. For example, in an attempt to manage their emotions, they may end up developing an addiction, which makes them even less resilient to the stress they are experiencing. They may also increase the traumatization of others by guilting and shaming those they see as perpetrators, ultimately becoming that which they are fighting.

Of course, it's important that people not use the fact that advocates can develop a post-traumatic response to witnessing atrocities as an excuse to pathologize or otherwise dismiss them. Many advocates suffer minimal traumatization and are able to manage their experience without contributing to dysfunctional relational dynamics. Advocates do the largely thankless and invisible work of cleaning up the mess created by others. Blaming them for having a natural psychological response to witnessing horrific atrocities is like blaming someone for getting dirty while they're mopping up another person's spill. The purpose of illuminating the trauma narrative is to help thwart the re-creation of nonrelational dynamics within the very systems that are designed to transform them.

Decreasing the Power of Narratives through Increasing Awareness

Humans are meaning-making animals, driven by narratives and destined to continue creating them. So we are always operating in the midst of narratives: to step outside of one narrative, we must already have adopted a different one.

Challenging nonrelational narratives, then, requires replacing them with alternative stories. But how do we determine which narratives to believe in? How do we distinguish fiction from fact?

The first step is to change the way we relate to narratives— both dominant and personal ones. This means maintaining an ongoing awareness of the existence of narratives, so that we don't automatically buy into them. It also means being committed to critically examining narratives—asking the right questions when we hear or create a story, such as what facts it's based on and how we can trust that those facts are accurate. For instance, are the facts produced by a reputable source, who, among other things, is not invested in maintaining or growing a power imbalance? Changing the way we relate to narratives also means looking for alternative explanations for what we may have accepted as "truth," in that we try to disprove the underlying assumptions driving the narrative. Changing the way we relate to narratives also involves examining our internal experiences—particularly when we're in a disadvantaged position—to see how we're affected by the narrative. For example, does the narrative cause us to feel shame? When the narrative is about our own experience, does it clash with our self-perceptions, our understanding of ourselves and, perhaps, our group?

Perhaps most notably, we need to assess whether a given narrative is ultimately nonrelational or relational. Does it serve to increase or rectify a power imbalance? in other words, does it involve a story about moral superiority and inferiority, or does it reflect integrity and honor dignity? Of course, even when a narrative *is* relational, it isn't guaranteed to be accurate. However, when a narrative is nonrelational, its *in*accuracy is pretty much a given because such a narrative is based on a mythology of defensive distortions.

When we reflect on the narratives in our world and lives, we are better able to interrupt the dynamics of oppression and to improve our own psychological wellbeing.

7

PRIVILEGE: PROTECTING INJUSTICE

When you're accustomed to privilege, equality feels like oppression.
—Anonymous

"Why?" asks attorney-activist Kimberlé Crenshaw to the sea of faces undulating around the little red dot that marks the center of the island she's standing on as she delivers her TEDWomen speech.[1] "Why does a frame matter?" She's discussing the 1976 class-action discrimination suit led by a Black woman named Emma DeGraffenreid against General Motors for segregating its workforce by both race and gender. "After all, an issue that affects Black people and an issue that affects women, wouldn't that necessarily include Black people who are women and women who are Black people?" Crenshaw (who was mentioned in Chapter 2) explains that how you answer this question depends on your frame. Emma's suit was dismissed because although GM in fact did not hire Black women, it *did* hire Black people and it *did* hire women: it hired white and Black men for maintenance and industrial jobs, and white women for reception and secretarial jobs. But the policymakers at GM and the courts didn't have a frame for—or an understanding of—how those who were both Black *and* women formed a distinct social category that caused them to be subjected to a distinct form of oppression. Crenshaw coined the term *intersectionality* to describe this intersection of oppressions, providing a new frame that has helped lay the groundwork for understanding and challenging privilege.[2]

But what exactly is privilege?[3] In nonrelational systems, privileges are advantages that are granted to powerholding groups or individuals and denied to others. Privilege, the third defense of nonrelational systems, keeps some people invested in maintaining power over others and makes it easy for them to do so, as privilege increases the likelihood that they will be successful in life and will have more power—more ability to influence and control others. At the same time, withholding privileges from, or disadvantaging, those with less power decreases the likelihood that these individuals will be successful or able to influence or control others. The more privileges we have, the more successful and powerful we tend to become and the more often we get the message that we're worthy, boosting our belief in our ability to accomplish what we set out to do. And the more we have been disadvantaged, the less likely we are to succeed or to believe in ourselves.

Privileges therefore help to ensure that nonrelational systems are self-perpetuating. For example, someone who was born into economic privilege is more likely to be healthy (thanks to access to wholesome nutrition and medicine) and well educated; to have strong networks that provide them with career opportunities promising power and influence; and to be encouraged to believe in themselves, which research shows is a key determining factor in success.[4] By contrast, the opposite is true for someone who was born into economic disadvantage.

A useful analogy for understanding privilege likens it to an intergenerational relay race. Those born into positions of privilege—economic, racial, gender, and so forth—start out close to the finish line, whereas those who are born into disadvantaged positions start behind everyone else, having to work harder to try to get ahead and often ending up unable to lessen the gap.[5]

Privilege is the final defense of nonrelational systems. Narratives and psychological defenses work together to create a mental lens that can distort our perceptions of reality to the point that fictions become facts and we defend the indefensible. Privilege both adds to psychological distortions and provides a structure with which they become systematized and actionable and through which they become integrated into not only our consciousness but also our policies and practices.

Practical and Psychological Privilege and Oppressive Systems

Privilege is maintained on both a practical, or structural, level and on a psychological level. *Practical privilege* and *psychological privilege* are woven together to create an ignorance of, investment in, and even dependence on the unjust power imbalances that mark nonrelational systems.

Practical privilege is the set of benefits that results from the myths of nonrelational systems being established as policies and protocols, and from the institutionalization of practices that sustain unjust power imbalances. For example, on a practical level, certain policies and legislation prevent people who are not cisgender from marrying, benefiting from tax reductions, or immigrating to another country when they're in an international relationship. Psychological privilege is the mentality that results from the myths that obscure and justify privilege being turned into narratives that teach us to buy into the very assumptions and attitudes that help the structures of privilege remain unchallenged. For example, the narrative that transgender and gender-nonconforming people are "deviant" and therefore not deserving of the same rights as cisgender people has prevented cisgender and non-cisgender people alike from challenging unjust legislation and policies.

The practical privileges granted to members of dominant groups in oppressive systems (as well as to powerholders in abusive systems in some cases) are countless, and they are in effect even before birth. For example, nutrition and stress affect fetal development and maternal mortality rates, and these factors are directly related to how much access a mother has to proper healthcare and support, which is in direct proportion to her socioeconomic status, particularly in countries like the US, where such services are largely privatized.[6]

However, many, perhaps most, privileges are psychological, and the advantages they afford—or the lack thereof—shape our lives and society in powerful ways. As we've discussed, nonrelational narratives teach us, for instance, to think of ourselves as attractive or unattractive, as worthy or unworthy—as better or worse than others. In one study, researchers gave five-year-old Black girls two dolls, one white and one Black, and asked them to say which one they preferred. Most girls chose the white one, saying that the white doll was "nice" while the Black one was "bad."[7]

When we have the privilege of seeing our experiences more accurately reflected and validated in mainstream culture, we learn to see ourselves as more nuanced and capable. Consider how representations of white people's experiences dominate the popular media and reflect complex (rather than simplistic or stereotypical) white characters and white struggles. White people (especially economically advantaged, cisgender heterosexual men) learn, for instance, that even if they do bad things, that doesn't necessarily make them bad people. They learn that the things that cause them distress—such as having to manage the demanding workload that comes with attending a private university or with corporate leadership—are indeed distressing and that their reactions to these challenges make sense. In short, when the mainstream culture reflects and validates our experiences, we get the message that our experiences matter. We learn that our dreams are valid and that if we try to achieve them, we can. We learn that our thoughts, feelings, and desires are more valid and more normal than those of others. We learn that we're more worthy.

Of course, we are more than just the roles we play in nonrelational systems. So we may be privileged but still feel powerless in many ways. This is because in a world governed by nonrelational systems, our deeper, authentic needs are rarely met. Nonrelational systems prevent us from relating to ourselves and others in the ways we need to in order to cultivate the kind of genuine connection and closeness that would bring a sense of satisfaction and true empowerment. Our privilege makes us feel compelled to maintain our privileged status, and although it enables us to get some of our needs met, fulfilling those needs always comes at the expense of others. And as long as we have bought into the tenets of a system that defines "enough" superficially, based on what we have rather than on who we are, we can never feel quite secure in ourselves. Nonrelational systems ultimately harm all of us by conditioning us to relate to others and ourselves in inauthentic, dysfunctional, and destructive ways.

The Three Key Features of Privilege

Privilege is like a cognitive impairment that hampers our ability to think objectively and to act compassionately. Privilege is distinguished by three key features: it allows those who have it to take up space, it is invisible to those who have it, and it is rarely examined or relinquished without resistance.

People with Privilege Take Up Space

One implicit rule of nonrelational systems that is expressed through privilege is that people with privilege are allowed to take up the space of others: they feel entitled to cross another's or others' boundaries. Boundaries are the lines delineating our physical, mental, or emotional space—our personal space. All living beings have boundaries, and when those boundaries are not respected, suffering and harm can result.

There is a wide range of ways in which we cross boundaries. We cross physical boundaries when we tell our partner what they can or can't wear; when we stand too close to someone or subject them to our loud music; when we invade and occupy others' land; when we dump toxic wastes into rivers and streams; or when we take the fur and flesh of individuals from other species to use for our own benefit. We cross psychological boundaries when we tell another or others that their perceptions are wrong, thereby invalidating their thoughts, opinions, or observations; or when we dominate a conversation and take up all the verbal space. We cross sexual boundaries when we engage in sexual street harassment, such as by making "cat calls," or when we try to coerce those with less power to engage with us sexually. We cross emotional boundaries when we tell another person that they're overreacting when their emotional response isn't what we think it should be.

When we have privilege and cross another's boundaries, we are usually unaware of this fact, and if we do become aware of it, we typically don't see our behavior as problematic. We may even feel offended by those who point out our boundary violation. For example, it's likely that few men realize the discomfort or distress that their "cat calls" elicit, and when the woman on the receiving end responds by asking them to stop or even by ignoring them, they may take offense and turn to sexist insults such as "bitch," essentially reasserting—rather than reflecting on—their male privilege. Likewise, when someone visits a friend who has a new kitten, even if the kitten is huddled in the corner of the room, fearful of being handled, the guest may nevertheless grab her, completely unaware that they are violating her boundary.

However, we tend to notice it immediately when our own space is invaded. For example, when someone stands too close to us or touches us when we haven't invited physical contact, or when someone revs their motorcycle outside our bedroom window as we're trying to sleep, we often have an instantaneous awareness of such a boundary violation, even though the person crossing our boundaries is probably oblivious to it.[8]

Privilege Is Invisible to Those Who Have It

Because most of us are unaware of our privilege, despite the fact that we all have certain privileges and therefore a certain amount of power, we don't actually *feel* powerful.[9] In fact, many of us feel that we don't have enough power, especially if we are struggling in our lives, financially or otherwise. When others try to point out our privilege to us, highlighting our white privilege or male privilege, for example, and asking us to relinquish some of it, we can feel misunderstood and react defensively. If we don't feel powerful, how can we be expected to "give up" power in a system that seems unfairly balanced against *us*?

One way to appreciate that it's possible to have privilege and still feel at a disadvantage is to imagine, as blogger Sian Ferguson suggests, that we're on a long bicycle trek with a friend and that we have different types of bikes and take different routes. Our friend's bike is a three-speed, whereas ours is a ten-speed. Our friend's route is all uphill, whereas ours is only sometimes uphill. The fact that our friend has a harder time than we do doesn't change the fact that the journey is hard for us, but it also doesn't mean that we and our friend suffer equally or face the same obstacles.[10]

We rarely become aware of our privilege until something forces us to truly grasp the experience of those who have less privilege than we do. Many of us from economically advantaged communities, for example, don't see the privilege we have until we travel through a community where we witness the poverty in which many people are forced to exist. Before we had this experience, we may have actually felt as though our lifestyle was substandard, having compared ourselves to those with a standard of living above ours, such as the celebrities and television characters whose lifestyles are held up for all to see and strive for. And the greater the number of dominant groups we belong to, the more our privilege feels normal and natural—as simply the way things are and the way things are meant to be. In the same way, the more we live among others in our privileged circles, the more normalized our lifestyle becomes and the more invisible the bubble we are in. So a paradox of privilege is that the more of it we have, the less we see it. Once we've become aware of our privilege, we can begin to examine it. Examining our privilege means developing a deeper understanding of its nature, expression, and particular manifestations in ourselves. This enables us to change our relationship with our privilege so that we don't use it to reinforce oppression; and instead, ideally, **we use it** in the service of social transformation.

Privilege Is Rarely Relinquished Willingly

One reason why privilege is difficult to challenge is that the nonrelational narratives that maintain privilege teach us to believe that all, or nearly all, privileges are earned and are therefore just. So when privilege *is* questioned, the act of questioning is seen as *un*just and is met with anger. This anger is defensive in nature; it emerges in order to defend privilege. So those with privilege feel entitled not only to their privilege but also to their privilege not being questioned. One hallmark of privilege is feeling entitled not to see or examine it.[11] Indeed, otherwise open and fair-minded individuals can become defensive to the point of utter irrationality when a particular privilege they hold comes into question. This defensiveness makes it especially hard to raise awareness of and discuss privilege and therefore to work toward transforming nonrelational systems.[12]

Defensive reactions are marked by a lack of curiosity and, perhaps most notably, a lack of empathy. When we're defensive, we're in a state of heightened arousal, meaning that our fight-flight-or-freeze response is activated and we have less access to our prefrontal cortex, which, as noted, is the part of our brain that's responsible for rational thinking.[13] This automatic response helps keep us alive; it's an instinctive reaction to danger that enables us to immediately deal with a threat. However, it doesn't serve us when what's needed is rational self-reflection. When we're in a state of defensiveness around our privilege, we also tend to fill space (and invade that of others) with our own opinions, feelings, and sense of righteousness rather than create space for learning and understanding. We are less likely to give others the benefit of the doubt and more apt to cling to narratives that serve to maintain a nonrelational dynamic that privileges us at the expense of others. This is one reason why people who have little to no literacy regarding systemic oppression and the privileges they have been afforded feel entitled to tell those who have such awareness that the latter don't know what they're talking about. And it's why these same people fail to recognize the utter hubris of this behavior.[14]

Our defensiveness often continues unchecked, in large part because we fail to see it for what it is. Our privilege distorts our perceptions so that we genuinely believe we're knowledgeable and open when, in fact, we're uninformed and unreceptive. Our privilege causes us to feel more literate than we actually are about the oppression it defends, and (as with dominant narratives) to mistake fact for opinion and opinion for fact. For example, a nondisabled manager who's asked to make changes to meet the needs of an employee suffering from depression, and who has no professional experience dealing with mental illness, may nevertheless insist that such changes are unnecessary. The manager may believe themself to be far more informed about the nature of depression and the needs of those suffering from it than they actually are. And even when the individual with depression and the mental health professional who advocated the changes for that individual provide clinical information about depression, the manager may treat these facts as opinions and their own opinions as facts, rendering productive dialogue impossible. This conflation of the subjective and the objective is why some privileged individuals use their own personal experiences to invalidate those of millions of others, as when a man who was raised in a family of "strong women" or who has struggled to get dates insists that women have more social power than men do. Our privilege can make us feel entitled to dismiss or ignore an entire issue, or even a justice movement, based simply on our own anecdotal experience.

In many ways, privilege is the glue that holds nonrelational systems together. And privilege is what causes some of the very people who might otherwise work to transform such systems to end up supporting them. Privilege is one of the central factors that prevent logical discussion and maintain widespread injustice. Without our realizing it, our privilege causes us to defend, rather than challenge, oppression.

The Myth of Meritocracy

The assumption that the privileges granted to powerholders are based on merit rather than luck—that they are earned rather than inherited from an unjust system—is central to keeping nonrelational systems intact. This *myth of meritocracy*—the belief that ability and hard work are always fairly rewarded—causes members of dominant groups to feel deserving of their success and members of nondominant groups to feel that their lack of success is their own fault, and it keeps everyone from seeing that the system is set up to maintain privileges and power imbalances that benefit some at the expense of others. Consider, for example, how members of socioeconomic groups who struggle to feed their families tend to believe that their own shortcomings are the reason for their hardship[15] (when they haven't been encouraged to blame a convenient scapegoat such as immigrants). If they were to recognize the real reason—the fact that they are on the losing end of a system that's unfairly rigged—they would probably feel angry at the injustice of their circumstances rather than blame themselves and feel ashamed.

The myth of meritocracy is also the foundation on which neoliberal ideologies and policies—those that favor free-market capitalism—stand, and when this myth is exposed and recognized, it becomes clear that neoliberalism is unlikely to lead to a more just and equitable social order. Indeed, while the main objective of progressive social policies is to help offset the power imbalances inherent in oppressive systems, by offering subsidies and other supports to lessen the gap between members of privileged groups and those who haven't been privileged, neoliberal policies typically seek to remove such provisions.

A fundamental difference between left- and right-wing thought is that the left tends to recognize the role of systems in general, and of oppressive systems in particular, in shaping social dynamics. Naturally, people with this understanding are more likely to support a political orientation that reflects it.

Often, however, critics on the right reverse this cause-and-effect equation. For example, it is not uncommon for these critics to argue that social science departments—a source of legitimation for progressive policies—are influenced by a left-wing bias. This argument is based on the fact that most faculty in the social sciences identify as left-leaning[16] and that most social scientists accept oppressive systems as legitimate social phenomena. The right-leaning critics' argument reflects the assumption that social scientists' progressive orientation causes them to believe in the existence of institutionalized power imbalances that unjustly privilege some at the expense of others—that the reason social scientists accept systems of oppression as valid is that they are left-leaning in the first place. However, the opposite is far more likely to be true: social scientists' understanding of systems of oppression is what leads them to support progressive politics. Consider Galileo, who, following in the footsteps of his predecessor Copernicus, argued against geocentricism (the belief that the other planets and the sun revolve around Earth) and for the progressive theory of heliocentrism (the belief that Earth and the other planets revolve around the sun). It was not Galileo's progressive orientation that caused him to support heliocentrism; rather, it was his scientific understanding that led to his progressive orientation.

Decreasing the Power of Privilege through Increasing Awareness

If we want to help transform the dynamics of privilege and oppression, we need to change our relationship with our privilege. And one essential way to do this is to become literate around privilege.[17]

When we're literate around privilege, we know the facts about privilege (about the nonrelational system any given privilege defends, such as classism, and about the structure of privilege itself), and we understand the meaning of those facts. We also empathize with those who are impacted by our privilege. We're *aware*; awareness is both an intellectual and an emotional state. We are therefore better able to recognize the subtle manifestations of oppression that can be difficult to detect, such as men's tendency to leave emotional labor[18] and other "caregiving" work, like providing food and drinks at and cleaning up after events, to the women in a mixed-gender office; or Westerners' tendency to avoid eye contact with Muslim women wearing a hijab, rendering the latter invisible. When we have an understanding of the nature of privilege, we are more likely to accept that we have unseen biases and are less likely to try to defend them.

Moreover, if those of us promoting a countersystem don't understand the nature of nonrelational systems in general (beyond the specific oppressive system we are targeting), we risk recreating problematic nonrelational dynamics in our outreach, turning natural allies to our cause away from it. For example, if white feminists promote an agenda that doesn't account for the experiences of BIPOC girls and women, the white feminists end up not only reinforcing racism but also failing to attract many people who are naturally allied with feminist values. And just as vegan advocates can develop gender, race, and class analyses so that they don't use sexist, racist, or classist messaging or approaches in their outreach, so too can feminists examine their own carnism so as to reduce, or ideally eliminate, their support of nonhuman animal exploitation as they work to end the exploitation inherent in patriarchy. Although we obviously have limited time and energy and cannot be active in all causes at once, we can commit to ensuring that our own work supports that of other movements, or at the very least that it doesn't come at a cost to others.

For those of us in powerholding positions, making a commitment to continuously growing our awareness of our privilege is a critical step to take if we hope to help transform nonrelational systems. As rational and straightforward as this suggestion sounds, though, few of us actually heed it, because the nature of privilege is such that it causes those who have it to deny or defend it. Awareness of the defensive nature of privilege can help fortify us against its corrosive influence.

PART 2

ENDING INJUSTICE

Relational Systems and Dynamics

Justice anywhere is a threat to injustice everywhere.

8
RELATIONAL SYSTEMS: THE ARCHITECTURE OF JUSTICE

Every thought you produce, anything you say,
any action you do, it bears your signature.
—Thich Nhat Hanh

THERE IS A BUDDHIST ADAGE that says we all have within us the seeds of greed, hatred, and desire, as well as the seeds of love, compassion, and empathy. Our job is just to water the right seeds. In other words, what we attend to will grow.

Ending injustice requires the dismantling of nonrelational systems and the transformation of nonrelational dynamics on all three levels—societal, interpersonal, and intrapersonal. To this end, it's important to understand the structure and nature not only of nonrelational systems and dynamics but also of their alternatives—relational systems and dynamics. With this understanding, we can be more intentional about which seeds we choose to water.

Relational Systems

Relational systems,[1] as we discussed in earlier chapters, are organized around the formula for healthy relating. Whereas nonrelational systems are closed systems that are dependent on myths and defenses and that invalidate anything that challenges their status quo, relational systems are open systems that welcome examination from within and outside themselves and that are structured to grow and evolve. While nonrelational systems are based on the power over model and the belief in a hierarchy of moral worth and are structured to maintain unjust power imbalances, relational systems are based on the power with model and they honor the dignity of all beings and are structured to balance power.[2] Relational systems are organized around behaviors and qualities that are the opposite of those that are oppressive and abusive.

Sometimes, relational systems are countersystems, such as feminism[3] or veganism—systems that emerged in reaction to oppressive systems. Other times, a relational system may have developed independently of an overtly oppressive system, as with Buddhist monk Thich Nhat Hanh's Order of Interbeing, a system that emphasizes collectivism, compassion, and curiosity.[4] Regardless of how they emerge, relational systems differ from nonrelational systems in both content (their focus, or objective) and process (how their proponents relate and communicate).

To summarize, relational systems are organized around the principles of honoring dignity, balancing power, and practicing integrity for the wellbeing of individuals and for the greater good. For example, the US civil rights movement was founded on the beliefs that people of all races and ethnicities have the same inherent worth and that power should be assigned equitably among members of different racial and ethnic groups. The movement was also founded on the belief that racist attitudes and practices are antithetical to the integrity of individuals and of society as a whole.[5]

Pseudo-Relational Systems

Certain nonrelational systems look like relational systems because they have the content that one would expect from a relational system, even though their process is nonrelational. So although such systems may have the stated goals of, for instance, balancing power and increasing integrity, their structure and dynamics are nonrelational. Proponents of these *pseudo-relational systems*[6] are rarely aware that the content and process of such systems are not aligned. However, recognizing these systems for what they are is important if we hope to avoid perpetuating nonrelational dynamics.

The following table shows the key features that differentiate a nonrelational system from a relational system.

Nonrelational	Relational
Power over	Power with
Disconnection	Connection
Insecurity	Security
Disempowerment	Empowerment
Shame/grandiosity/contempt	Pride/humility
Competition (win-lose)	Cooperation (all-win)
Violates integrity	Reflects integrity
Unjust power imbalances	Just distribution of power
Harms dignity	Honors dignity
Relational dysfunction	Relational health

Violates boundaries	Honors boundaries
Fosters insecure attachment	Fosters secure attachment
Trauma	Love/resilience
Hierarchy of moral worth	All equally morally worthy
Closed system	Open system
Based on myths	Based on awareness

Fundamentalist Systems

Fundamentalism is the strict adherence to a set of basic principles (a set of beliefs with associated values) that have been interpreted literally and narrowly. It is characterized by the rejection of diversity of opinion or interpretation.[7] Beliefs are typically seen not as beliefs, but as ultimate truths. Fundamentalism is therefore not so much about the content of a system as it is about the process. It is not about specific beliefs but about the process of relating to those beliefs.

In a fundamentalist system, one either agrees with the accepted beliefs and is "right" or does not agree and is "wrong." Fundamentalists don't think, "We have different beliefs," but rather, "Your beliefs are wrong." Whereas facts can be objectively right or wrong, accurate or inaccurate, beliefs are, by definition, subjective. They are conclusions based on an understanding and interpretation of facts. Clearly, certain beliefs are more grounded in and supported by factual accuracy than are others, but when we talk about beliefs as being right or wrong, we are inevitably making moral judgments, not statements of fact.

Fundamentalism therefore creates a perception of "us versus them" and places "them" on a lower rung of a perceived moral hierarchy. Indeed, fundamentalists are ideological purists, and when ideological purity is a core value, then anything that deviates from it tends to be perceived as defiled, degraded—as morally inferior. Fundamentalist systems are based on nonrelational principles and practices.

Fundamentalist systems are sometimes formed by groups within justice movements that split off from existing, established channels, often because of ideological or strategic disagreements. These groups tend to be more radical than the mainstream movement, but radicalization does not automatically translate to fundamentalism. It's understandable how fundamentalist systems end up forming: proponents of countersystems are often those who have been harmed by an oppressive system, whose beliefs and values have been chronically invalidated, and who have consistently felt shamed and silenced. They may need to create a strong in-group identity to assert their position and to adhere more intensely to their values and beliefs. However, regardless of why a fundamentalist system develops, whenever nonrelational behaviors are used to challenge nonrelational behaviors, we end up with more of the same.

Traumatic Systems

Sometimes, a countersystem can evolve into a "traumatic system," particularly when the nonrelational system being challenged causes extensive violence. Proponents of the countersystem can develop post-traumatic stress from experiencing or witnessing the violence,[8] and the traumatic dynamics they end up engaging in can easily turn the aspiring relational system into a nonrelational one. Indeed, trauma is contagious: traumatized people often relate to others in such a way as to trigger them to also develop symptoms of trauma.[9]

Symptoms of post-traumatic stress include chronic workaholism, emotional numbing, dysregulation (feeling emotionally out of balance and experiencing intense emotions that are difficult or impossible to manage), oscillation between the extremes of emotional intensity and numbing, intrusive thoughts, misanthropy, survivor guilt (feeling guilty for having survived a traumatic event while others perished), a sense of shame and/or grandiosity, and burnout. Perhaps most notably, post-traumatic stress can lead to the development of a trauma narrative, which, as we discussed in Chapter 6, causes us to perceive and relate to the world as though it were divided into victims, perpetrators, and heroes and to treat others and ourselves accordingly.

Many proponents of countersystems who have been traumatized struggle with feeling that they are not good enough and not doing enough to stop the suffering, and in an attempt to offset their guilt and shame, they neglect their own needs. Attending to one's needs, though, is essential for becoming resilient—resilience is the ability to withstand and bounce back from stress, traumatic or otherwise—and ultimately for maintaining a sense of connection.[10] Indeed, resilience is often built and practiced in community. However, those with unaddressed trauma often relate to others in a way that weakens the others' resilience (by shaming them or encouraging them to overwork, for example), which can create a vicious cycle of nonrelational dynamics that eventually leads to the creation of a nonrelational system.[11]

There is much overlap between traumatic and fundamentalist systems. One could even say that a traumatic system is a type of fundamentalist system, though not all fundamentalist systems may necessarily be traumatic.

Pseudo-Relational Systems and Distorted Perceptions of Power

Sometimes, a nonrelational system presents itself as a relational one because its purported goal is to balance power—which is one key aspect of relational systems—even though its actual underlying goal is to maintain or increase an existing power imbalance. Proponents of these pseudo-relational systems no doubt rarely, if ever, realize that they already have what they're fighting for—or that acquiring more power won't bring them the sense of empowerment or self-worth they seek, as it's impossible to feel truly empowered and worthy in such a way within a nonrelational system.

For example, white supremacists who feel disempowered by the fact that the power differential between white people and BIPOC has finally begun to lessen (even though the imbalance remains significant) perceive the shift in race relations as a total overturning of "white power": they actually see white people as being on the lower end of an unbalanced power dynamic.[12] Similarly, some men seek to establish "all-male clubs" simply because there are "all-female" environments.[13] They assume that measures to create safety (emotional and/or physical) for a group with far less social power and far higher rates of gender-based victimization reflect a total reversal in the gender power differential.

These pseudo-relational systems reflect inaccurate assessments of how power is concentrated and distributed. They are based on distorted perceptions and a lack of data. One way to challenge such systems is to conduct an analysis of the current power distribution—to evaluate which group holds more positions of influence in social institutions, has more ideas represented throughout those institutions, and wields more economic power—and to assess the historical trend of the power distribution—to determine how long the current dominant group has been the powerholder. This data can be used to encourage proponents of the pseudo-relational system to recognize that their perceptions of power are skewed and to reflect on their existing privilege. Of course, shifting perceptions will take more than presenting data analyses, but gathering accurate information to challenge "false facts" is an important step in the right direction.

We Become What We Do

Gandhi famously said, "As the means, so the ends." In other words, the process used to accomplish a goal will shape the goal itself. Proponents of nonviolent social change have long championed the approach of using a healthy process to challenge an unhealthy system, believing that we become what we practice. And from a psychological perspective, Gandhi's claim makes sense.

Ending injustice requires not simply abolishing nonrelational policies and practices but transforming nonrelational systems—and, as we have noted, such systems are psychological in nature. A system is made up of a network of relationships, and relationships are made up of people, and people are psychological beings. Every action we engage in, including thinking, reflects a way of relating, in that the action can be relational or nonrelational. And every action that is reciprocated becomes an interaction, or a dynamic. Systems, whether they comprise two or two million individuals, are essentially aggregates of dynamics. Moreover, nonrelational behaviors are contagious. When a nonrelational behavior is enacted, it almost inevitably triggers a nonrelational response. Therefore, as we've been discussing throughout this book, if we hope to end injustice, we need to change the way we relate.

In her groundbreaking book *Dignity*, author Donna Hicks cites myriad studies demonstrating that we are hardwired to respond to affronts to our dignity—which are inherent in nonrelational behaviors—as though they were assaults on our body.[14] Studies have shown that emotional pain, including the pain of feeling shame (which results from harmed dignity), has a similar effect on our brain as does physical pain. In other words, the brain doesn't know the difference between a harm to dignity and a harm to the body: the pain caused by shame is as real as physical pain. Neuroscientists, using fMRI scans to observe brain activity in people as they were put through different scenarios, found that "when someone was feeling a psychological [emotional] injury [e.g., if their feelings were hurt], it showed up in the same part of the brain as a physical injury [e.g., if their leg was hurt]."

When our dignity is harmed, we go into a state of hyperarousal, and as we noted in Chapter 7, our capacity for rational and empathic responding is diminished. Indeed, as mentioned in Chapter 3, our automatic tendency is to counterattack, often in a like manner. Among the studies cited by Hicks is one by James Gilligan, who asked twenty-five hundred inmates why they had felt compelled to kill; the majority said that it was because they had felt disrespected.[15]

In *Emotional Intelligence*, author Daniel Goleman points out that on a neurobiological level, we are powerfully impacted by relational dynamics. Interactions that cause us to feel demeaned can actually weaken our immune system and over time can even reshape our brain.[16] Multiple studies have demonstrated that the way we express ourselves toward another—including through microexpressions that are often not even consciously detected by either party—causes the other to respond in kind.[17] The studies also showed that it takes five "positive" or relational communications (in which we're being affirming or supportive, for example) to offset a single "negative" or nonrelational one (in which we're being offensive or invalidating).[18] Indeed, just one nonrelational communication, such as an insulting email we receive, can diminish our mood and energy level for hours or even days.[19] Some emotional-contagion researchers claim that negative (nonrelational) interactions "spread like the common cold."[20] So nonrelational dynamics beget nonrelational dynamics on many levels—psychological, behavioral, societal, and even biological. Over time, if we engage in nonrelational dynamics enough in our personal and social systems, they become normalized, and our systems can become nonrelational. Herein lies the reason why the process is so vital, why the means do indeed powerfully inform the ends when we're working toward transforming oppression.

The tendency for nonrelational dynamics to recreate themselves is also why social problems cannot be solved simply through technological or even rational means. Although technology can certainly play a role in the creation of a more just world, without a shift of consciousness from nonrelational to relational, technological innovations can be, and often have been, used to sustain nonrelational systems. The internet, for example, both empowered Al Qaida and helped mobilize the Arab Spring uprisings. And although rationality is critical to ending oppression, rational solutions to problems of oppression that are conceptualized from within the nonrelational mindset can easily lead to conclusions that support, rather than challenge, nonrelational systems.

Indeed, when we challenge a nonrelational system by using nonrelational tactics and dynamics, the content of that system may change, but the process does not. It can be helpful to think of the nonrelational mentality as an entity with a survival instinct (a metaphor akin to that used in Chapter 6). To feed itself, this mentality needs an "other," another individual or group deemed less worthy. It doesn't care who that other is. The other exists simply to keep the mentality alive—to maintain the sense of superiority of the powerholding individual or group—and to preserve the power imbalance.[21] So as long as nonrelational dynamics are a system's norm, they will find an outlet somewhere. The individuals or groups being victimized by the nonrelational system may change, but the nonrelational dynamics remain intact.

As we work to end injustice, situations will inevitably arise in which we have to ask ourselves whether, in some cases, our approach must incorporate actions that appear nonrelational. We may need to enforce power over individuals or groups that are causing harm to others in order to, for example, prevent hate speech. However, even in those circumstances, we can maintain a commitment to relationality, by trying to ensure that our actions honor the dignity of the individuals being impacted and are in the best interests of the greater good—that they are designed not simply to reduce harm but also to increase integrity and balance power. For instance, people who promote and implement policies and legislation that prevent hate speech can keep their focus on preventing harmful behavior rather than on curtailing "immoral people." Indeed, experts point out that many people join hate groups in their youth, while they're still impressionable, and that among members of these groups, the incidence of childhood physical abuse and psychological maltreatment is higher than average.[22] There are many reasons why individuals are attracted to hate groups, but a key driver is the search for a sense of connection, belonging, power, and personal value. Christian Picciolini, white-supremacist leader turned peace activist, contends that filling these needs and extending compassion to such individuals (while still holding them accountable) are essential to transforming their violent mindset.[23] Further affronts to their dignity would no doubt feed their sense of disconnection, disempowerment, and hate, causing them to feel even more defensive and attached to nonrelational systems and to further obstruct justice.

On a practical level, there will be knotty problems to unravel as we work toward change. The needs of different individuals and groups will clash, and what is in the best interests of the individual or of the greater good may sometimes be difficult or impossible to determine. But if we approach social change with a commitment to practicing relationality, we will be far better able to address these problems in a productive manner that leads to sound solutions.

It's also important to note that not only do nonrelational dynamics beget nonrelational dynamics, but having power begets nonrelational dynamics. Having power tends to corrupt: it distorts our perceptions of ourselves and others, such that we often act nonrelationally without realizing that we're doing so. So it's important to understand how power affects us, including how having or acquiring even small amounts of power can alter our thoughts and feelings, driving us to engage in dynamics that reflect the nonrelational power over model. Research has shown, for example, that when we're in a position of power, we experience diminished empathy, are less likely to act with integrity, and are more likely to act in self-serving, entitled, and impulsive ways and to justify these behaviors to ourselves and others.[24] If we're not aware of the corrupting influence of power, when we work to challenge nonrelational dynamics, we risk simply inverting the hierarchical ladder of moral worth.[25] For instance, after holding accountable a powerholding executive of an NGO who'd harassed staff members, the non-powerholding staff can start to bully other, nonoffending executives by keeping them under constant threat of being targeted as abusive even when they're not.

The Corrosive Nature of Shame

Nonrelational behaviors are contagious in large part because they are shaming. And most of us have been taught to use shaming behaviors toward a variety of ends, including (among other things) to navigate disagreements, manage our feelings of disappointment and frustration when our efforts aren't successful, handle our survivor guilt, get others to change what we see as problematic behaviors, get our needs for recognition and appreciation met, and bolster our sense of self-worth. Perhaps not surprisingly, then, shaming behaviors are a key reason why a purportedly relational countersystem could morph into a nonrelational one. When shame is used as a tool to manage the issues that proponents of the countersystem inevitably encounter, it can easily corrode the system.

In a countersystem whose goal is to help end some form of injustice (e.g., animal or environmental exploitation), it's all too easy for proponents to resort to shaming behaviors toward those whose support they're trying to attract—as well as toward those within that very system—in order to achieve their goals. For example, vegan advocates might shame nonvegans for enabling animal exploitation, and climate advocates might shame other climate advocates whose strategic approach to promoting sustainable policies the former disagree with. Such shaming behaviors can become increasingly normalized and, over time, cause the system to become nonrelational.

Despite the problematic nature of shaming behaviors, many advocates nevertheless use shame in hope of bringing about change. So it can be helpful to understand the science of shame. What the research shows is that there are not, as many people believe, two kinds of shame—"toxic" and "helpful." All shame is toxic: shaming someone is assigning a negative label to a person rather than to an action, and it creates relationally dysfunctional outcomes. As mentioned in Chapter 3, research also shows that shame has an inverse relationship with motivation to change. In other words, someone who's being shamed is more likely to resist change than to be open to changing. Feeling shame also increases the chances that someone will engage in behaviors that harm themselves and/or others, such as abusing drugs or alcohol or developing eating disorders.

It makes both rational and intuitive sense that shaming others isn't an effective way to encourage them to change. If we're asking someone to change a behavior that we perceive as unethical or "wrong" (e.g., voting for racist policies or using genderist language), we're asking them to reflect on the fact that what they're currently doing isn't in alignment with their moral values. In so doing, we're asking them to be open to seeing the ways they have been contributing to harm and to sit with the feelings that accompany such awareness. One of those feelings is guilt, which often automatically morphs into shame. We're asking people to stop justifying a behavior and to experience the feelings that result from dropping their defenses. We are asking them to be the opposite of defensive—to be vulnerable.

As such, we're more likely to be able to hold people accountable if we create an environment in which they can authentically reflect on their harmful behaviors and feel willing and able to rectify them. As Brené Brown, arguably the leading researcher on shame, points out, "to be accountable you need to be vulnerable."[26] How can we expect someone to be vulnerable with us if we don't show them that it's safe to do so?

Relational Behaviors Are Contagious

The good news is that, as noted, relational behaviors, like nonrelational behaviors, are also self-replicating.[27] What this means is that the more we engage in relational behaviors, the healthier our systems, and we ourselves, become.

Indeed, we each have the power to help shift the systems of which we are a part. In Chapter 4, we noted that systems are like dances, and that in order for a system to function, all members have to be dancing to the same song, doing the same dance steps.[28] We cannot dance with a partner who is waltzing if we're doing the foxtrot. The dance steps, of course, are the roles and rules of the system in which we're operating. To change the dance, we must change our own dance steps—the roles we play and the rules we follow. Obviously, we have different amounts of power to bring about change in different systems. For example, in a partnership, with all power roles being relatively equal, we have much more power to shift the system than we do in a social system. However, when enough individuals in a system change their dance steps, the process of the system is interrupted, and ultimately, the system transforms.

9
RELATIONAL COMMUNICATION: THE EXPRESSION OF JUSTICE

When we focus on clarifying what is being observed, felt,
and needed rather than on diagnosing and judging, we
discover the depth of our own compassion.
—Marshall B. Rosenberg

BECAUSE NONRELATIONAL BEHAVIORS ARE CONTAGIOUS, spreading with every relationally dysfunctional interaction, it's important that we commit to building relational literacy as we work toward broader social transformation. Promoting compassion and justice in our social outreach while, for example, shaming those who disagree with us on social media sites or belittling our partner is a bit like being an environmentalist who drives a Hummer.

This is not to say that we are entirely responsible for transforming all of the nonrelational systems that we're challenging and/or by which we are being harmed, or that we should strive for moral perfection. It's also not to imply that we all have an equal opportunity to practice relational behaviors. We need to have at least some degree of privilege in order to be able to choose how we act, and those with more power to change a system have a greater responsibility to do so. Rather, it's to suggest that if we want to create a world in which people feel less compelled to demean others and are better able to practice integrity, we need to construct a base of dignity on which to build healthy interpersonal and social relationships. Part of this work entails integrating relational dynamics into all areas of our lives to the best of our ability, through building relational literacy, which, as we discussed, is the understanding of and ability to practice healthy ways of relating.

There are a number of principles and tools for building relational literacy, and I've dedicated an entire book, *Getting Relationships Right*, to the subject. Here, we'll look at one of the most essential components: practicing relational communication.

Communication is the primary way we relate. What this means is that nonrelational communication is the primary way we act out relationally dysfunctional dynamics. When we understand how to shift a communication from nonrelational to relational, we're much more empowered to help shift all our dynamics and systems.

Also, because we're communicating virtually all the time, with others and with ourselves, we have myriad opportunities to build relational literacy; we can use our communication as a training ground on which to build our relational muscles. We can practice relational communication when, for example, we're discussing a difference of opinion with our partner, when we're posting a political commentary online, or even when we're sitting and quietly reflecting on our day. Indeed, studies have shown that our internal dialogue impacts many aspects of our experience, such as our self-perception and our ability to achieve our goals. Pausing to notice and, when appropriate, restructure our self-talk so that it's more relational can significantly improve our wellbeing and relationships.[1] (Working on our internal dialogue may be particularly important when we're occupying disadvantaged positions in a system, because we may have internalized oppressive messages about ourselves.)

Focus More on the Process
than the Content of a Communication

Relational communication encompasses the formula for healthy relating and basic effective communication principles and tools. Perhaps the most important of these principles is to be more process- than content-focused. Every communication (every interaction, in fact) has two parts: the content and the process. The content is what we're communicating about, and the process is how we're communicating. We tend to overfocus on the content, but the process matters more. If you think of a conversation that you had several months ago, you may well have forgotten the entire content—what you actually talked about. But you probably still remember how you felt during that conversation. The process—how we communicate—determines how we feel.

A healthy process looks the same regardless of what we're communicating about—whether we're discussing if we should stay in or go out on a Saturday night, for example, or we're making the case for using the third-person singular "they" in our outreach materials. When our process is healthy, it reflects the formula for healthy relating: we practice integrity and honor dignity, which leads to a greater sense of security and connection. So the goal, or agenda, of our communication is not to win or to be right (which means making the other person lose or be wrong). Rather, the goal is mutual understanding—to understand and be understood. Even when we're speaking as advocates of a cause and we want people to be receptive to our message, our first and primary goal needs to be mutual understanding.

A process is often not fully healthy or unhealthy; rather, it can be more or less so. The healthier our process, the more respectful it is to both ourselves and the other person. The less healthy our process, the less respectful it is. When our process is healthy enough, no matter what the content of our conversation, no matter how different our opinions and needs may be from one another, we can discuss just about anything openly and honestly—and we can deepen the security and connection in the dynamic. Conversely, when our process is not healthy enough, no matter the content of the conversation, we'll likely end up arguing and weakening the security and connection in the dynamic.

It is at the level of process where nonrelational ways of communicating (and, more broadly, of interacting) are either reinforced or transformed, both internally and externally, on both the personal and the societal levels. When therapists work with families or couples in distress and when political mediators work with leaders of states in conflict with one another, their main job is to facilitate the process of communication between the different parties so that healing and reconciliation may begin. Focusing on the process rather than the content of communication takes a conversation out of the realm of ideas and brings it to the deeper level of how people relate to one another—about not only ideas but also everything else, including needs, feelings, and experiences.

Discuss Rather than Debate
Generally, when our process is healthy, we discuss rather than debate. Debating rarely leads to the outcomes we want. The debate model works in only a handful of situations, such as in a courtroom or political forum. When we debate, our goal is to win and therefore to make the other person lose. Debating is a

counterproductive and nonrelational form of communication in the vast majority of circumstances.

We can easily fall into debate mode when we're dealing with differences of opinion, as we tend to focus primarily or entirely on the content without paying attention to the process. We try to convince the other or others of the rightness of our position and end up increasing both their and our defensiveness. When people debate an issue, they can become more attached to their own viewpoint rather than open to others. They are motivated to try to avoid "losing" the argument and to come up with all the reasons as to why their position is right, convincing themselves of the validity of their position in the process.

A Roadmap for Relational Communicating

In their excellent book *Messages*, authors Matthew McKay, Martha Davis, and Patrick Fanning present a useful tool for effective communicating: whole messages.[2] Whole messages are based on the principles of nonviolent communication[3] and are designed to prevent the expresser from defining reality (believing or acting as though they are an expert on another individual's experience, as we discussed in Chapter 6), to create an atmosphere of objectivity, respect, and trust.

Whole messages contain four parts: observations, thoughts, feelings, and needs. Not all messages will require the expression of all four parts, of course, but this formula can be applied in any situation where it's especially important to ensure that communication is clear.

When we express our observations, we share what we have observed with our senses—what we've seen, heard, and so on. Observations are reports of objective facts, not speculations, interpretations, or conclusions. For example, an observation may be, "It's 90 degrees Fahrenheit," or, "I left my phone at home today," or, "The official language of France is French."

When we express our thoughts, we share our conclusions or perceptions based on our observations. Our thoughts are our subjective interpretations, and they may include our value judgments, beliefs, or opinions. For example, a thought might be, "Relationships take work," or, "Denmark has an interesting political history."

When we express our feelings, we share our emotional experience. You might say, for example, "I feel ashamed of what I said to you yesterday," or, "I'm so happy and grateful that you're coming to the talk on career development with me; it really means a lot to me to be able to share the experience with you." Often, we say "I feel" when we really mean "I think." For example, you might say, "I feel like more and more people are attacking others on the internet these days," when you're actually expressing a thought.[4]

When we express our needs, we communicate what we want or hope for. Many of us are ashamed of having needs and have never learned how to articulate them, so we try to get our needs met through indirect means. However, expecting others to meet our needs without our having communicated them clearly is unfair, and it's a recipe for disappointment and conflict. To express a need, you might say, "Could you stop by the grocery store on your way to the office? I'd really love to have snacks available for the team meeting, and we're all out," or, "When you said that you wouldn't go to the Caribbean festival with me and the kids on my birthday, I felt like you made a unilateral decision that affects the whole family. Can we put aside some time this evening to talk about this?"

Like observations, thoughts, and feelings, needs should reflect *your* experience, so expressing your needs should not include blaming or judging another. In addition, expressed needs should be concrete and direct, and it should be possible for the person to whom you're expressing your needs to meet them.

When we use whole messages, we immediately reduce others' defensiveness and are better able to have a rational, compassionate conversation. Additionally, we train ourselves to become self-observers and more mindful, intentional communicators. By trying to figure out what's an observation (for example, that it's 90 degrees) and what's an interpretation (that it's hot), we learn to think more objectively and to avoid unfairly making others responsible for problems they haven't caused; and we learn to pause and reflect before we communicate. In other words, we learn to develop self-awareness and practice mindfulness, two of the most fundamental elements of relational literacy.

Developing Self-Awareness and Practicing Mindfulness

Developing self-awareness and practicing mindfulness both reflect and reinforce relational communication and, more broadly, relational literacy. The more self-aware and mindful we are, the less likely we are to be hijacked by automatic defensive reactions to nonrelational dynamics—to catch and spread the contagious virus that is these dynamics—and the more likely we are to practice integrity and honor others' (and our own) dignity.

Self-Awareness

Self-awareness is the understanding of and capacity to reflect on our thoughts, feelings, personality, identity, resources, and other aspects of our personal and internal experiences. Studies have shown that high levels of self-awareness are integral to healthy relationships, and to effective leadership,[5] an issue that pertains to all of us who are organizers and ambassadors for social causes.

If we don't know ourselves—including what kinds of behaviors or events cause us to become defensive and dysregulated,[6] what deeper motivations drive our actions, and so forth—and if we don't know what we're thinking, feeling, and needing, we're unlikely to be able to relate to others or ourselves in a way that's healthy and productive.

How can we attend to ourselves or communicate to others our thoughts, feelings, and needs if we don't even know what those thoughts, feelings, and needs are in the first place? How can we make sure our choices and communications are respectful if we don't recognize when we're dysregulated?

When we're more self-aware, we are

- better able to recognize and therefore attend to and communicate our needs, including our relational needs (the need for reassurance, connection, or respect, for example), so we are less likely to engage in controlling or manipulative behaviors to get our needs met
- more likely to identify our boundaries, and therefore less likely to allow others to violate them
- less likely to act out defensively, as we're more open to self-examination and can reflect on and learn from our feeling of defensiveness without reacting to it
- more likely to be accountable when we engage in nonrelational behaviors that harm others and to rectify such behaviors, because we're open to self-examination
- more in tune with our core moral values, so we're more likely to know when we're not acting in accordance with them
- more honest with ourselves and open to examining our beliefs, so we're less likely to think dogmatically and more likely to make behavioral choices that reflect what we

authentically think and feel, rather than what we've been
taught to think and feel

- more likely to appreciate how our experience is different
from that of others, so we're less likely to assume that
others should think, feel, and act as we do and to judge
them for being different

Mindfulness

Mindfulness is both a practice and a state. It is at once a tool for
developing awareness and a state of presence, of being present in
the moment.

Multiple studies have demonstrated that practicing
mindfulness increases self- and other-awareness and improves
relationality.[7] Practicing mindfulness actually rewires the brain
so that we become less defensive and more attentive, focused,
empathic, and compassionate.[8] What's more is that it enables us
to better observe and regulate our emotions to prevent ourselves
from getting triggered into hyperarousal. And when we do end up
triggered in this way, we're better able to self-soothe and reduce our
hyperarousal so that we regain access to our prefrontal cortex and
are better able to think rationally and reconnect with our empathy.
Practicing mindfulness also increases resilience, which, as we've
noted, is the ability to withstand and bounce back from stress, and
it ultimately enables us to be more intentional and less automatic
and reactive in our interactions.

Mindfulness can be practiced through any activity, from eating
to walking to doing household chores. Two activities that can be
especially powerful ways to practice mindfulness are relational
communication, as we've noted, and meditation. Both of these
methods help cultivate our "inner observer," the part of ourselves
that objectively and compassionately witnesses our experiences as

they unfold. As our inner observer becomes stronger, we create more space in ourselves so that we're not automatically impacted by and reactive to either internal stimuli, like our thoughts and feelings, or external stimuli, like others' behaviors. We can therefore approach situations more rationally and compassionately.[9] (To develop your inner observer, it can be helpful to set an alarm to go off several times throughout the day and pause to nonjudgmentally reflect on your inner experiences—to ask yourself what you are thinking and feeling.)

There are a number of methods for developing a meditation practice. Today, many apps and programs make the process easier than it used to be, and you can tailor your practice to your needs. (A particularly useful app is Waking Up by Sam Harris, which is based on Harris's book of the same name. The app provides not only meditation guidance, but also guidance on how to move beyond mindfulness to truly "wake up" and live a more examined and enlightened life.) According to research, meditating for even ten minutes a day can help develop mindfulness.[10] It's also worth noting that in some cases, meditation is contraindicated. For example, people who have experienced trauma and who have not yet established a sufficient sense of internal safety may find that meditation worsens their symptoms.

How to Evaluate Whether a Communication Is Nonrelational or Relational

Even with the knowledge of what relational communication is, it can be difficult to differentiate it from nonrelational communication, especially when the dysfunction within the communication is subtle. So, to try to determine whether a communication is nonrelational or relational, you can ask yourself the following questions:

- How would I feel if I were on the receiving end of the communication? or, How do I feel [if the communication is directed toward you]?
- Is the person communicating someone I would feel safe being vulnerable with?
- Does the communication reflect integrity and honor dignity? Put differently, does it reflect civility?
- Would I feel safe expressing an opinion the person communicating would disagree with?
- Would I direct this same communication toward someone I care about?
- Is the person communicating framing the conversation as a divisive debate (e.g., are they pitting one person or idea against another in a "versus," win-lose framework)?
- If the person is communicating debate-style, is the person they are debating actually present?

Another strategy to help you assess how relational a communication is, is to think of someone whom you consider to be relationally healthy. A relationally healthy person is self-aware; curious (open-minded); responsive rather than reactive (they reflect on what they'll say or do before acting); tuned in and responsive to the experience and needs of others (they consider how their behaviors will impact others and act accordingly); authentic (they're honest and, when appropriate, vulnerable—for example, they are able to admit they've made a mistake, make an apology, or say "I don't know"); and compassionate. In other words, this is a person of integrity. Ask yourself: Would this person engage in the kind of behavior I'm witnessing?

Eventually, as your own communication becomes more relational, you probably won't need to go through this list of questions. The more relationally literate you are, the more repelled you'll feel when you encounter nonrelational behaviors. The process of becoming relationally healthy is similar to the process of becoming physically healthy. Imagine that you quit smoking and stop eating highly processed, fatty and sugary foods, and then you take a drag of a cigarette or eat a bag of donuts. The substances your body once found gratifying it now recognizes as toxic. You feel poisoned, which you essentially are. Likewise, you may find that you "outgrow" some of your relationships and that, over time, you choose to be a part of systems that are healthier and more nourishing.

10
RELATIONAL ROLES: TRANSFORMING OPPRESSIVE SYSTEMS TO ACHIEVE JUSTICE

All you need to know is that the future is wide open
and you are about to create it by what you do.
—Pema Chödrön

ALTHOUGH POPULAR CULTURE—AT LEAST in many parts of the world—has taught us to believe in the nonrelational myth that we can and should be islands unto ourselves, in truth, we are all interconnected within the various systems of which we are a part. We're like spiders running along the strands of a great web of interbeing, every seemingly independent action affecting, and being affected by, the whole. Given that we are participants within myriad systems—for better or worse—our choice is not *whether* we participate but *how* we participate. When we understand how to participate in a way that transforms nonrelational systems, we can be part of the process of ending, or moving beyond, oppression—oppression being, as we've noted, the most notable driver and manifestation of injustice.

Moving beyond oppression requires not only a shift of consciousness and dynamics, from nonrelational to relational, but also a commitment on our part to making specific changes based on our role, or position, and our intention within a given oppressive system. In this chapter, we'll discuss some ways we as individuals can help transform oppressive systems when we are in a powerholding, or privileged, position and/or when we are acting as advocates, challenging privilege from either a privileged or an oppressed position.[1] (Although collective measures, such as community organizing and political lobbying, are essential, whether and how to carry out such efforts need to be determined contextually; that process goes beyond the scope of this book.)

It's also useful to note that because oppressive systems are traumatic systems, the roles we play in an oppressive system may mirror those played in a traumatic event. When we are privileged, we may be in the role of "perpetrator"; when we are experiencing oppression, we may be in the role of "victim"; and when we challenge privilege, we may be in the role of "hero," and we can play the hero role from either of the aforementioned positions—that is, we can challenge privilege from a position of privilege by acting as an ally, or we can challenge privilege as one of those who is experiencing oppression.

Transforming Oppressive Systems When We Are Privileged

Transforming an oppressive system requires changing how we relate within the system. When we are in a powerholding position, we're in a position of privilege; so to end oppression, we need to change the way we relate to our privilege. We need to relate to our privilege such that we help offset, rather than reinforce, oppression.

Moreover, as noted previously, the onus for transforming oppressive systems must be on those in positions of greater power. When we are in a position of privilege, we generally have more power to change the oppressive system than we would were we in a disadvantaged position. And given that we've been benefiting at the expense of others, whether we've wanted this to be the case or not, our working on rectifying the unfair power imbalance is an important step toward creating a more just system.

Learning and Listening

When we're in a position of privilege, it's essential that we commit to developing literacy around privilege. It's also important that, as we learn, we not expect those from groups who are experiencing oppression to become our teachers.[2] Often, we can feel that our mere willingness to learn about our privilege is somehow an act of heroism and that those who are negatively impacted by our privilege should be grateful for the opportunity to try to educate us. Consider, for instance, how the one student who's a member of a particular nondominant group (Muslim, genderqueer, Torres Strait Islander, etc.) in a classroom may be expected to represent their entire community by providing their perspective on whatever topic is being discussed. This situation is often seen as an opportunity for them rather than a burden. Indeed, being open to learning about how our privilege has caused us to walk over the rights of others feels noble only because of the entitlement such privilege instills in us; the least we can do is look at what we need to see in order to stop causing harm. To this end, it's *our* responsibility to get educated. We are simply falling back on our privilege when we put others in the position of having to synthesize and communicate complex interpersonal and social dynamics and structures that they may not have fully thought through themselves, a task that would inevitably cost them significant time and energy. It's not fair to expect others to give us all the answers or to solve our problems for us. The information is out there for us to find on our own.[3]

Although we need to take care not to make others responsible for our education, it's important that we ask questions that help us understand the experiences of others who see our privilege more clearly than we do. Often, when those of us with privilege do ask questions, we do so only to create an opportunity to debate the answers we get and to further justify our privilege. We may pose hypothetical questions that have little bearing on the issue at hand, asking, for example, how the social order would be maintained if all people had satisfying jobs and earned living wages ("Don't we need people to do the work nobody wants to do?"). In this way, we use the conversation not as a forum for examining our privilege but rather as an opportunity to assert and defend it. We may feel that playing devil's advocate is the best way for us to truly understand an issue, but such an approach can easily cause those who have been chronically invalidated and challenged to feel that they are being cross-examined and that their reality is being doubted once again. When communicating with those who are negatively impacted by our privilege, it's especially important for us to adapt our conversational style such that it respects their experience.

We also need to accept that we do not and cannot know what another's experience is like unless they tell us, especially when they are a member of a nondominant group to which we don't belong— and that we very likely know far less than they do when it comes to their group's experience of power dynamics. Often, when the subject of our privilege comes up—when we find ourselves in a conversation about gender or race, for instance, and we belong to the dominant group—our tendency is not to listen and learn but to take on the role of expert, because our privilege causes us to think that we know more than we actually do about the issue at hand. For example, women often find that as soon as they begin to discuss their experience living in patriarchy, men start explaining all the ways in which the women are wrong about what they're perceiving, feeling, or wanting. Sometimes, men also point out how they have had the same experience, suggesting that there is no patriarchal power imbalance. When the #MeToo movement began, with myriad women speaking out against high-powered men by whom they'd been sexually harassed in a culture of rampant sexism and violence against women and girls, some men who had been victims of sexual harassment claimed it was likely that many men and boys had also been victimized but were simply not coming forward. This might be true, but the suggestion was nevertheless that sexual violence is somehow gender-neutral when it is a well-documented gender-based phenomenon.[4]

In short, we should be careful not to define the reality of members of nondominant groups, which is a tendency instilled by our privilege. When others point out our privilege, we need to listen to what they have to say, even if they don't communicate in the most gracious way. People don't always communicate as effectively as they could, especially when the subject is charged. Nevertheless, we need to listen and hold off on our tendency to try to make them wrong and poke holes in their argument so as to defend our own privileged position. We may not always agree with what we hear, but it's essential that we commit to doing our best to be fully open to the information coming our way. Of course, our willingness to listen should be within reason. Everyone deserves to be treated with basic respect, and if a conversation is demeaning or otherwise disrespectful—reflecting nonrelational dynamics—choosing not to engage may well be the choice of integrity.

So, we need to notice our tendency to feel defensive when we hear about how our privilege impacts others, and not act on this feeling. We need to know that it's the nature of privilege to cause us to feel attacked whenever we hear about it; to exaggerate the anger of those communicating with us; to fail to see their anger as a normal and healthy response to injustice; to deny or minimize their suffering or the injustice caused by our privilege and to grasp at arguments to prove them wrong; and to assume that our dominant narrative is more valid than their nondominant one, when the opposite is most likely the case.

Tailoring Our Communication

When we discuss our privilege with those who have been harmed by it, our usual ways of communicating are often not sufficient. This is largely because those individuals may have strong emotions, and possibly even post-traumatic reactions, around the issue. Their pain may be the result of the harm and suffering they've endured or, in some cases, witnessed. It may also result from their having been chronically silenced. Many individuals who try to speak out only to face the anger and defensiveness of the dominant, oppressive culture end up angry and defensive themselves. When people aren't listened to when they talk, especially about matters in which the stakes are high, they talk louder and eventually end up yelling. They can also fall into despair when productive conversation seems hopeless.

The intensity of the pain felt by members of groups that are oppressed can also be the result of years, even generations, of emotional repression being released. It's not uncommon for the painful emotions caused by oppression to be stuffed down, or repressed, at least to some degree, as long as there has been no tolerance or space for their expression. People often repress their emotions when they get the message that such emotions are "wrong"—that what they're emotional about isn't really happening or is their fault—and so they don't feel entitled to feel them. People may also repress their emotions when they believe that it's not safe or useful to feel and express them—when, for instance, they believe that they'll be assaulted for expressing their anger or that nobody will take them seriously, and so they assume that self-expression will cause them to feel even more enraged and despairing. This dynamic is perhaps easier to understand in the context of an abusive relationship. As long as the abuser refuses to acknowledge the injustice and harm of their behaviors, the person being abused cannot afford to (fully) feel their emotions that result from the abuse unless they are ready and able to end the relationship. Repressing emotions in order to function is a coping mechanism that enables people to manage remaining in the unhealthy systems that they are not free to simply exit.

Once there is an opening for repressed emotions to emerge, these feelings can come rushing to the surface. This can occur when the denial of those of us who are privileged is pierced, and we are able to acknowledge the pain that our actions or the actions of others who share our privilege have caused. At this point, those who have been harmed by our privilege are often still reeling from years of emotional, and sometimes physical, wounding; but we are not sufficiently literate, and we don't realize that our usual ways of communicating are not appropriate and can even be counterproductive. Such a phenomenon was common during the early stages of the #MeToo movement, when a number of men expressed a genuine desire to engage in productive dialogue but found that their attempts to communicate fueled the problem rather than offsetting it.

Because the usual forms of communication often don't work in dialogues about privilege and oppression, we need some guidelines for such conversations. Understanding the stages of recovery from trauma[5]—stages that may also apply to recovery from oppression—can help guide our communications so that they can be more productive.

Understanding Stages of Recovery from Trauma

Recovery from trauma is a complex process, with stages that are often revisited over time. Here, we'll just briefly define the stages for the purpose of understanding their influence on communication. The first stage of recovery is safety. Individuals or groups who have felt unsafe, emotionally or otherwise, and disempowered—hallmarks of both traumatic and oppressive experiences—need to know, first and foremost, that they won't be further harmed. In the second stage, they acknowledge and express the emotions related to the trauma (which is only possible if safety has been established). In the third and final stage, they reconnect with others, and it is only at this point that communicating with them in the usual ways is appropriate.

When an individual or group that has been oppressed first begins raising awareness of a powerholder's privilege, it is often during stage 1 or 2 of recovery; it is therefore not the time to employ the usual means of communicating, as not enough healing has taken place. This simply means that those of us in privileged positions should talk less and listen more. When we do talk, it should be primarily in the interest of learning more about the individual's experience (asking, for example, "What has it been like for you to experience this?"). As noted, playing devil's advocate or debating—even if we are truly on a quest for truth—may well cause the person to feel that their reality is being defined or to otherwise feel invalidated, as such behaviors mirror the very methods that have been used to maintain the oppression they're speaking out about. Looking again at #MeToo, we can perhaps better understand why many well-intentioned men who attempted to join the conversation felt frustrated at what they believed was an expectation that they stifle their curiosity and suppress their questions. These men ended up assuming that forums for discussion were preventing a diversity of opinions, and tensions escalated.

The early stages of an individual or group's recovery are also not the time for us to talk too much about ourselves, including about our own concerns regarding the problems our privilege has caused. If we self-reference in such ways, we can be perceived as, and can in fact be, placing ourselves back in the privileged position of being the focus of attention, of being "centered." Centering ourselves can also be seen as a demand for empathy. For many people who are members of groups that are oppressed, empathy for those who have contributed to the oppression (even if they haven't done so directly or intentionally) can be dangerous. As members of groups that are oppressed, they are socialized to over-empathize with members of privileged groups and to deny their own perspectives and needs.

In the early stages of recovery from oppression, our focus should be primarily on listening deeply, with the goal of fully understanding their experiences. Of course, it's important that we listen in this way in all of the stages, but by the third stage, listening can be accompanied more fully by other forms of communicating.

Transforming Oppressive Systems When We Are Acting as Advocates

We're in a position of advocacy when we're challenging privilege, whether we're doing so as members of the privileged group or as members of the group harmed by the privilege. Regardless of our power role, when we're advocating to transform oppressive systems, there are some strategies we can employ to increase the chances that our efforts will succeed.

Practice Compassionate Witnessing

All of us straddle multiple realities: we all have some forms of privilege, and we all belong to some groups that are oppressed. (Because oppressive systems include those involving nonhumans, even people who belong to multiple oppressed groups nevertheless retain human privilege.) Although certain methods for transforming oppressive systems discussed in this chapter are more appropriate and impactful when we employ them from a particular position we're occupying, most methods are still at least somewhat applicable regardless of our position. However, one method in particular is perhaps equally appropriate, regardless of our position: *compassionate witnessing*.

Compassionate witnessing, so named by psychologist Kaethe Weingarten, entails paying attention and listening with empathy and compassion, without judgment.[6] When we compassionately witness another, our goal is not to be right, to win an argument, or even to fix a problem. It is simply to understand the truth of the other's experience. In compassionate witnessing, we're saying, "I see you—I empathize and I care." This is what occurred during the process of truth and reconciliation in South Africa, and in the BBC program *Facing the Truth*, in which sessions between victims and perpetrators of Northern Ireland's political conflict were mediated.[7] Of course, compassionate witnessing in itself doesn't guarantee an ideal outcome of a situation, but it's a necessary step in the process of reconciliation or healing.

To be truly seen is to be given a great gift, one that is sorely lacking in most of our lives and in the culture at large. It is especially lacking among those who have less power in oppressive systems, as their experiences are underrepresented and misrepresented and are therefore rendered less visible or invisible.

Compassionate witnessing is a central practice of relationality. We feel validated when we feel accepted for who we are, when we don't feel judged for what we think and feel. And when we feel validated, we feel unashamed and worthy—we feel that we matter. Compassionate witnessing therefore prevents and transforms shame. When we're told that our feelings or experience are "wrong," or when we're not acknowledged or validated when we reach out to another, we get the message that we don't matter. By contrast, when we're met with compassion and empathy, we feel empowered, secure, and connected.

Compassionate witnessing can transform our lives and our world. When we compassionately witness ourselves, we deepen our connection with ourselves, and we enhance our integrity and decrease our shame. When we practice compassionate witnessing toward others, we empathize with those who are suffering and help create a kinder and more just world. Indeed, virtually every atrocity has been made possible by a populace that turned away from a reality it felt it could not or need not face. And virtually every social transformation has been made possible by a group of people who chose to bear witness and encouraged others to bear witness as well. Social transformation requires that we shift from a culture of oppression to a culture of compassionate witnessing.

Compassionate witnessing can also help us develop healthy psychological boundaries, which are essential for healthy interpersonal dynamics and relationships. Psychological boundaries enable us to be at once "connected and protected," in the words of relationship expert Terrence Real.[8] When relating within an oppressive system, members of powerholding groups tend to have boundaries that are too rigid: their boundaries don't allow in information that challenges their narrative or that enables them to identify and empathize with those whose experiences they have not been sensitized to. On the other hand, people who have been oppressed tend to have boundaries that are too porous: their boundaries cause them to distrust their own narrative when it competes with the dominant one and to over-identify and -empathize with others, especially powerholders. Therefore, those with less power often need to increase their self-witnessing so that they don't overfocus on others or allow others' version of reality to define their own.[9]

Be Careful with Calling Out

Sometimes, those of us who are members of groups that have been oppressed and/or are advocates for such groups can, in an attempt to shore up our boundaries, develop a reactionary psychological rigidity. As we strive to balance power, we may cling too rigidly to our own reactionary narrative about people who belong to dominant groups—about those people's motivations, character, internal experience, and so on. In so doing, we end up defining the reality of members of dominant groups, exercising power over them and invalidating and shaming them.[10] An example of this phenomenon is call-out culture,[11] in which attempts to raise awareness of oppression by pointing out instances of oppressive behavior, often using social media, are frequently carried out in such a way as to punish or chastise rather than to educate.

A number of concepts and terms have emerged to highlight and challenge the defensiveness caused by privilege. However, although these expressions are important means of initiating productive conversations, they often contribute to call-out culture. When the process by which these expressions are implemented reflects nonrelational rather than relational communication, it demeans those being asked to change their relationship with their privilege and puts them in a no-win situation. For instance, if a powerholder doesn't speak out in an online discussion about oppression, they may be told that they're hiding behind their privilege and that they're not an ally. If they do speak out—even if they make it clear they're speaking from the only position they can, that is, their own experience—they may be told that they're centering themself or, worse, erasing the voices of those with less power, and that they shouldn't be speaking. If, when they speak out, they make a comment that reflects an ignorance of their privilege, as all people inevitably do, their character may be attacked (they may be called racist, sexist, ableist, etc.). If they feel ashamed or hurt, they may be told that they are, for instance, "crying male tears" (that their shame is exaggerated or fabricated). If they explain their reasoning for an opinion or statement, they may be told they're being defensive. If they've been on the receiving end of disrespectful, inflammatory comments and they ask to be spoken to respectfully, they may be told they're tone-policing. (Note that tone policing is stating that a person should not communicate when they're feeling or expressing emotion; this is not the same as requesting that a communication be respectful, which is healthful and necessary for productive dialogue.) So we need to remember to allow others to be the experts on their own experience, lest we communicate that defining someone's reality and making otherwise disrespectful comments are acceptable behaviors—and lest we use the tools that were constructed to support relational dynamics as weapons to defend nonrelational ones.

Of course, call-out culture emerged in large part to counteract the culture of privilege that makes people feel entitled to say whatever they want and not get called on it. However, how we talk about privilege matters. No matter how "right" we may feel our countersystem is, facts are rarely sufficient to sell an ideology. Debating facts or simply stating the rightness of our position is unlikely to win us supporters. If we fail to appreciate the psychology of those with whom we communicate, we will likely increase their defensiveness rather than their awareness. For example, despite having acknowledged the fragility, or heightened sensitivity, of members of dominant groups when it comes to examining their own privilege, many justice advocates blatantly neglect to take this fact into consideration, calling out and shaming those who are most likely to react defensively to shame (and most people *are* fragile when being shamed). Rather than use this knowledge of fragility to inform more effective outreach, some advocates do the very things that tend to trigger shame and defensiveness. It's like holding a glass vase that's full of cracks and, instead of handling it extra gently, slamming it down and then getting angry when it breaks. If we hope to challenge privilege, we need to be especially careful to frame our message in a way that takes into account people's sensitivity around the issue.

Some readers may argue that attending to the fragility of members of dominant groups shifts yet another burden from those who are privileged onto those who are not, making the latter responsible for "coddling" the very people who already have unfair advantages. It can also be argued that many powerholders use their fragility as a way to avoid being held accountable for their actions. Their strong emotional reaction to having their privilege pointed out often makes others too uncomfortable to bring up the topic. These arguments are true. It is also true that if we hope to be effective in challenging privilege, we need to relate to people as they are, not as we wish they were. If we ignore psychological realities because we don't like such realities, we can sabotage our efforts for change. Furthermore, it's entirely possible to be gentle *and* firm when we challenge privilege. We can be cautious not to trigger shame while still holding people accountable and being clear about our demands, which is the respectful approach no matter whom we're relating to.

Is it fair that members of nondominant groups must work to bridge ideological and communication gaps to try to balance power? Of course not. But unlike powerholders, members of nondominant groups have lived in two worlds—their own world, and that of the dominant culture whose language they've had to learn in order to survive. So members of nondominant groups are essentially fluent in two languages, while members of dominant groups are fluent in only one. On top of this, members of nondominant groups are often motivated to bring about change to a degree that most members of dominant groups simply are not.

Resist the Compulsion to Shame

Many advocates resort to shaming as a tactic not only because they believe that shame will motivate people to change, but also because they underestimate the consequences of shaming powerholders. (As we've discussed, studies have shown that shaming behaviors—which are those that harm dignity—trigger a defensive response that reduces the likelihood that a person will be open to making positive changes.[12])

Many of us assume that there's an inverse relationship between power and vulnerability: that the more power someone has, the less vulnerable they are to feeling shame. This is often not the case, and sometimes the opposite is true. From critics who publicly shame celebrities to employees who talk degradingly about their supervisors, the people engaging in these shaming behaviors tend to do so because they assume that the powerholders in question are somehow immune to such attacks. However, just about nobody is immune to the toxic and debilitating effects of shame. Even "punching up" can deliver a harmful blow.

Don't Indulge Contemptuous Moral Outrage

The ethos of the culture in which communication now takes place, most of which transpires online, has become such that we not only tolerate but even celebrate contempt, particularly when it's expressed through moral outrage. Indeed, we have learned to embrace a toxic moral perfectionism whereby we hold others, and often ourselves, to impossible standards. Someone makes one unexamined or selfish choice or statement and they become the enemy, the morally inferior *other*. We rally around those who raise the battle cry of moral outrage and who wield power over others even as they call for justice and compassion, because we've learned to believe that abuse isn't really abuse as long as we hold the moral high ground. Such outrage can be intoxicating, as it has an addictive pull, so we need to be vigilant in our efforts not to be seduced by its siren song. We need to develop the self-awareness and presence that would enable us to notice and resist its attraction.

Anger is an appropriate and legitimate emotional reaction to injustice. However, when our anger has the charge of contempt, it drives us to act nonrelationally.

Call In and Create Allies

When we "call in," as referred to by blogger Ngọc Loan Trần, rather than call out, we invite others to be a part of the solution, even if they're not fully engaged with the cause we're advocating.[13] Perhaps most notably, we work to raise awareness of oppressive behaviors without shaming; we hold others accountable and still treat them in a way that honors their dignity.

Calling in is not only relational, but it's also strategic. In a democratic society, change at the societal level is brought about not only by a small group of core advocates who drive a countersystem, but by a critical mass of supporters who help tip the scales of power.

To attract popular support, advocates' messaging and interactions cannot be seen as "against" those whose support they seek to attract.

When we call in, we create allies. We give others the opportunity to support our cause even if they don't follow all the tenets of our movement. For example, vegan advocates can choose not to buy into the myth that someone is either vegan and part of the solution or not vegan and part of the problem. Vegans can appreciate that someone has another option—to be an ally to the cause, a supporter of vegans and vegan values who uses their influence to help transform carnism. A vegan supporter can, for instance, stand up for a vegan on the receiving end of hostile carnistic humor, speak out against carnism, and/or support vegan organizations and initiatives. Ideally, a vegan supporter makes choices that are as vegan as possible when it comes to their own consumption.

Tips for Communicating Relationally When We're Acting as Advocates

We discussed the basics of relational communication in Chapter 9. Here are some practical tips we can use when acting as advocates, to communicate in a way that increases the likelihood that our message will be heard and heeded.

Whenever possible, avoid absolutes. Absolutes are rarely accurate, and when we use them, we risk coming across as blaming all members of a group for the behaviors of some. For example, instead of saying that "men" or "wealthy people" do something, say that "many men" or "some wealthy people" do it.

Don't assume that you know the internal experience of the privileged person(s) you're communicating with or about. Don't make definitive statements about, for example, why they said or did something insensitive ("They're selfish," or, "They don't care") or why they are motivated to ask questions ("He's using his male privilege to center himself"). Although it's important to think critically about the conversational dynamics around privilege and oppression, allowing others to be the experts on their own experience is a generosity everyone deserves, and it's the opposite of the nonrelational attitude that reflects privilege.

Avoid character assassination. Calling someone a classist because they made a classist comment is conflating that person's character (which we can't know because we're not in their skin) with their behavior, and it's more likely to turn people off of a cause than to win supporters to it. So, for example, instead of saying, "You're a classist," you could say, "You made a statement that's classist."

Focus on observable behaviors, not on your interpretations of the behaviors. For example, rather than say, "She made an ableist comment and won't respond to my criticism about it, so that means she wants to hold on to the power that comes with her privilege," simply focus on the comment and the fact that the person didn't respond. Moreover, be careful to examine your assumptions about what you perceive as privileged behavior. Try not to automatically assume that someone's powerholding position is to blame for problematic interactions when other factors may be at play. For example, before assuming that male privilege is the reason your supervisor isn't acting on your recommendation, ask yourself if there may be other reasons for his decision. We need to be mindful to approach difficult situations with as much objectivity as possible so that we don't level unfair accusations or perhaps avoid accountability for our own behaviors, which limits our personal and relational growth.

Stick to the facts. Avoid hyperbole and communicate the facts as objectively as possible. For example, don't refer to someone's comments that offended others as "malicious." We can't know the intention of another (unless they've told us), so we can't know if the comments were intended to harm. Instead, refer to them as "statements that were experienced as offensive."

Make sure that the facts you're communicating are accurate. There are countless examples on social media of comments that appear to reflect unexamined privilege or unethical behaviors but that have been taken out of context or misconstrued and are accepted uncritically and disseminated unthinkingly. Such a lack of attentiveness to facts can devastate the people whose words or actions are being publicly displayed, as well as create fear and distrust in (sometimes millions of) onlookers.

Avoid sharing (or making) comments that are disrespectful or otherwise shaming. This includes comments that convey yelling, such as those using all capital letters and multiple exclamation points. Nonrelational communication is epidemic in large part because we don't hold the people propagating it accountable, as we tend to believe that the ends (e.g., social justice) justify the means. Be extremely skeptical of anyone who claims that it's ever appropriate to communicate without compassion and respect. As noted, by its very nature, the nonrelational mentality seeks to perpetuate itself and it continually constructs new and often elusive justifications toward this goal. One way to recognize nonrelational thinking in yourself is to ask yourself whether you're perceiving another as morally inferior and whether you're feeling the corresponding emotion of contempt.

When feasible, communicate with an individual privately rather than in public. Of course, there are times when publicly pointing out someone's privileged behavior can be useful—such as when the person is a celebrity and is not personally accessible, when they're communicating a problematic message that needs to be publicly countered, or when they've engaged in bullying or violent behavior (e.g., sexual harassment) that makes them a threat to others. However, many people who make offensive statements are simply unaware of their privilege and they end up being publicly reprimanded when critical feedback shared in private would have been both more respectful and likely more strategic, as it doesn't make you come across as insensitive. Regardless of whether you're giving feedback privately or publicly, it's important to communicate respectfully.

Stay connected with your empathy (if you feel safe enough to do so). Imagine the expression of the person with or about whom you're communicating as they read or hear your communication. Frame your message so that it honors their dignity, even as you point out the problems their privilege causes. If you feel unsafe remaining empathic, worried that you'll lose your own perspective if you're too open to the other person's, then you might need more time to heal and shore up your psychological boundaries before speaking out about the issue.

Speak to the person, not to their privilege, assuming goodwill. It can help to remember that people are more than just their privilege, and that "good" people engage in harmful behaviors and that doesn't make them "bad." Believing that a person's problematic behavior means that they should forfeit their right to be treated with basic respect is precisely the kind of thinking that's caused the nonrelational problems in the world we're attempting to change.

Make sure the goal of your commentary is to raise awareness and bring about positive change, and ask yourself whether your communication is helping to achieve this end. If your goal is to be right or to express your anger, your communication will no doubt reflect this intention and be unproductive or even counterproductive. Of course, you *may* be right, and you may well have a right to be angry. It's simply important that these feelings not be ends in themselves.

Avoid reductive thinking. When we appreciate that we are all complex beings who are more than just our identities and whose behaviors don't define us, we're better able to relate to others in a way that's authentic and effective. We're better able to avoid what I refer to as "reductive thinking"—reducing an individual or group to nothing more than a behavior or set of behaviors. For example, if you're driving and are aggressively cut off by another driver, you're probably not thinking of the driver as an otherwise thoughtful person who's racing to the hospital for an emergency or who's just distracted by the radio and isn't paying attention. You're probably not thinking of them as a person who has hopes and fears, who's loved and lost. They're just "the jerk driver." You've reduced them to nothing more than this one behavior.

Likewise, we can reduce someone to "the bigot," "the conservative," or "the sellout." We'll therefore likely communicate that their "bad" behaviors or beliefs mean they're a "bad" person, harming their dignity and reducing the chances that they'll be open to our message.

Making sure the roles we play and the communication methods we use are relational may seem like drops in the bucket when we think about the enormity of the challenge of transforming oppression. But these approaches can be gamechangers, and they can go a long way toward helping us end injustice.

11

THE RELATIONAL METAMISSION: BUILDING RESILIENT, UNIFIED MOVEMENTS FOR JUSTICE

There's strength in numbers. Once we show the world that we're together, they can't stop us.
—Cory Hardricht

A RECENT STUDY FOUND THAT for any large-scale movement or initiative to change social norms, it needs to be supported by 25 percent of the population. This is its tipping point. So if our goal is to end injustice, to transform nonrelational systems, we need to attract a lot of people.

In order to reach this goal, we need to ensure that our movements (and groups) working for justice are as effective as possible. This means that they need to be resilient. A resilient movement is powerful and impactful; first and foremost, it's relational. As such, it's internally unified.

In a resilient movement, advocates feel secure and connected with one another. Because communication is clear and respectful, advocates are able to express differing and even dissenting opinions without fear of recrimination, such as being shamed and marginalized within the movement. Advocates are also more likely to be critical consumers and producers of information, with the ability and willingness to assess the validity of their own and others' opinions, as well as to employ change strategies (the methods they use to encourage others to shift their attitudes and behaviors) that are effective. And they are more likely to stand in solidarity with other justice movements.

A movement that's not resilient reflects the opposite. Perhaps the most notable element of such a movement is that it tends to be plagued by infighting. Infighting is both a reflection and a driver of low resilience. The problems that fuel infighting—such as a prevalence of burned-out, misanthropic advocates who end up either becoming increasingly ineffective or quitting the movement altogether—also cause or are exacerbated by infighting.

Infighting is highly toxic to a movement. It undermines the morale of individual advocates and of teams in organizations and groups, and it can substantially hurt their performance. It increases the chances that advocates will suffer from post-traumatic stress, turns potential supporters away from the cause, is a key driver of burnout, and prevents the kind of open-minded, critical analysis and discussion necessary for building a truly strategic and inclusive movement. Infighting bleeds much-needed resources from a movement, sucking up tremendous time, energy, and money. For example, a 2019 report revealed that dysfunction among staff ("toxic work cultures") cost US businesses $223 billion over the previous five years.[1] And research has shown that just one person who engages in "toxic behaviors" in a group can reduce the group's productivity by 30–40 percent.[2] In short, infighting causes our movements to cannibalize themselves.

Many advocates are aware of the harm caused by infighting, and for them, witnessing this problem is sometimes even more painful than witnessing the injustice their movement is working to end. As we witness infighting, we can feel like we're a part of a crew on a lifeboat, surrounded by individuals who are drowning and trying to save as many as possible, while some of the other crew members shoot holes in the bottom of the boat. We can feel betrayed, having thought that our fellow advocates were on our side but then learning that even those who advocate justice and compassion are sometimes neither just nor compassionate. And we can feel deeply frustrated as we watch others in our movement fighting among themselves, while the atrocity we're trying to end continues unhindered.

Most advocates do not engage in the highly toxic, nonrelational behaviors that drive infighting. But it only takes a vocal minority of advocates in a movement to create an infighting epidemic, and often these advocates are unintentionally enabled by advocates who don't recognize the nonrelational behaviors for what they are. So one of the most important ways to build resilient movements is to understand and address infighting.

The good news is that we're not helpless to end the problem of infighting or to build more resilient, unified movements. A key reason why infighting continues is simply that we haven't fully understood its causes and how to address them.

What Infighting Is

Infighting is, in many ways, the same as what we could call "outfighting"—as any kind of fighting—except that it's directed toward members of one's own group. What this means is that the very attitudes and behaviors that drive advocates apart are those that drive others away from advocates' message. They are also the same dynamics that enable injustice more broadly. So when we understand how to stop infighting, we also understand how to more effectively advocate to end injustice—and how to better contribute to a more just world.

In general, we fight when we have a difference of opinion or need, and we use force to try to get the other individual or individuals to change. In other words, we use an aggressive strategy to influence others to change in a particular way.

What Infighting Is Not

Infighting is not in-disagreeing. Disagreements about all sorts of issues, from philosophy to strategy to values, are essential for creating a diverse, thoughtful, robust, and impactful movement.

A healthy movement is, in many ways, like a healthy individual— constantly growing and evolving. A healthy person regularly self-reflects and critically examines their assumptions, updating those assumptions if they no longer fit in with new understanding. Likewise, a healthy movement is made up of advocates who question the movement's assumptions and behaviors and challenge it to grow and progress.

Some of these challenges are particularly important, as when women and BIPOC speak out against imbalances of power in a movement. We need to be careful not to refer to these kinds of challenges (or to any kinds of healthy challenges that are helping a movement evolve) as "infighting," or we could be weaponizing the concept and silencing critical voices.

In-Bullying

Often, what we refer to as infighting isn't infighting at all because what is happening is not actually a fight. A fight implies that there are two or more sides attacking each other. In many cases, we see one party using their power, their platform, to attack another, which is essentially bullying, or *in-bullying*. In some situations, the person(s) being bullied will retaliate in self-defense, but even then, the problem remains more one of bullying than one of actual fighting.

Bullying can be devastating, and it can be even more so when done by someone in our own inner circle, on our own team, and when its focus is on something that we care deeply about, like preventing other beings from being oppressed and tortured. Bullying can cause people to develop a range of psychological problems, not the least of which is traumatization. And trauma, which is already epidemic among justice advocates, is a leading cause of ineffective advocacy, burnout, and many other issues that significantly reduce the impact of our efforts and weaken our movements.

Whether the problem we're dealing with is in-bullying or infighting (for our purposes, I'll refer to both as infighting), the result is the same: harm to our movements and ourselves.

Key Causes of Infighting

There are a number of causes of infighting among advocates; the following are what I believe to be the key ones.

- Most advocates haven't learned to build relational literacy, so they're relating to one another in a way that's dysfunctional.
- Advocates don't always act as critical consumers and producers of information, and can, for example, buy into and spread disinformation that harms organizations or leaders within a movement.
- Being aware of and trying to end an atrocity psychologically impacts many advocates, such that they buy into certain beliefs and adopt certain behaviors that divide them from one another.

- The change strategy (the approach to encouraging others to change) that many advocates have learned to use is counterproductive.

Of these, relational dysfunction is undoubtedly the primary driver of infighting, and it also exacerbates the others (the less relationally literate we are, the more likely we are to be impacted by the other factors that contribute to infighting). Since we've discussed relational dysfunction and literacy at length, and since the critical consumption and production of information goes beyond the scope of this book, we'll just address the final two factors in this chapter. (See **endinfighting.org** for a comprehensive compilation of materials.)

The Psychological Impact of Being Aware of Injustices
Those of us who are aware of and working to offset the consequences of injustices—most notably, the harm and suffering that mark oppressive systems—are often psychologically affected by this reality. We can buy into certain beliefs or develop certain tendencies that contribute to infighting (and also to outfighting).

Believing That If We're Not United, We're Divided
A common belief among advocates is that if we're not united, we're divided. One reason we hold this belief is that we are often portrayed by the dominant culture as a one-dimensional, homogeneous group (e.g., a feminist is a feminist and all feminists are the same), and we can internalize this perspective, even though we know better.

Like members of other nondominant groups, we as advocates can also feel pressured to present a unified front in order to prevent our differences from being used against us in the common divide-

and-conquer strategy used by nonrelational systems to maintain themselves. For example, we can feel that we have to agree on everything and always get along in order for our demands and needs to be taken seriously.

It's important for advocates working to end any kind of oppression to remember that advocates are people and people are different from one another. Those of us who are in a movement for justice are no less diverse than those who aren't. Sharing a set of values doesn't mean we can or should have everything, or even a lot of things, in common. The beliefs and values that lead us to challenge oppression are but one aspect of who each of us is, one part of a complex whole—as is our occupation or religion or marital status, for example.

This belief that if we're not united, we're divided can cause us to feel triggered by our differences and to feel that we have to quell or even squash them. But when we relate to our differences in a healthy way, rather than fighting among ourselves, we embrace our diversity and can create a more resilient, impactful movement.

Believing That Differences Are Problematic

The belief that if we're not united, we're divided reflects and reinforces another inaccurate belief, which is espoused not only by advocates but by pretty much everybody: that differences between people, particularly those who are a part of the same system, are inherently problematic.

Rather than appreciate that differences are normal, natural, and necessary, we believe that those who don't share our beliefs, values, tendencies, strategic approach, and so on are somehow "wrong" and need to be changed to be more like we are. Of course, not all ideas are equally applicable to furthering a movement, and not all strategic approaches are equally effective. However, the main problem is not our differences, but the way we relate to our differences. We can't determine which ideas are most relevant or which strategies are most effective if we are unable to discuss those differences openly.

Differences and Debates

When we haven't learned how to relate to our differences in a healthy way, our disagreements can become divisive debates that limit our ability to effect change. Debating prevents us from engaging in the constructive conversations that would allow us to determine which of our ideas, strategies, and so forth are most useful and to develop new, synergistic ways of understanding and approaching a situation.

Debate is based on and, indeed, encourages dualistic, either-or thinking. In a debate we are often forced to choose between two opposing views and can therefore fail to see the many alternative views that may exist. We can also fail to appreciate the nuances of an issue, or that there may be multiple, equally valid interpretations of the same situation.

Discussion, or dialogue, on the other hand, is based on sharing ideas and becoming aware of multiple perspectives. The goal is for each party to understand and be understood by the other. Through dialogue, we are encouraged to examine our own assumptions, consider the limitations of our perspective, and contemplate alternative explanations or courses of action for the issue we're exploring.

In many ways, our diversity is our strength—the more ideas and experiences we bring to our movement, the richer and more multidimensional it becomes. When we truly appreciate the value of differences, we can cultivate the kind of productive dialogue that enables us to explore the most expedient methods with which to stop the tide of horrific injustice perpetrated against other beings. This tide does not pause while we argue with each other.

Ingrouping

Ingrouping is the psychological process of creating a strong social identity around a particular group we belong to, and feeling morally superior to those who don't share our identity. Ingrouping causes us to think in terms of "us versus them," and it reflects and reinforces the perception of differences being inherently problematic.[3]

Advocates often create a social identity based on their cause because it helps them feel more securely anchored in their beliefs. Calling yourself an environmentalist, for example, may help you hold true to your environmental values when you're feeling pressured to go on that gas-guzzling road trip to Disney World with your family. So holding on to a social identity can be a way we help ourselves feel safe in the midst of pressures and offensives from the dominant culture.

A social identity becomes problematic when we become too strongly attached to it or when it becomes value-laden, as is the case with ingrouping. Those of us who are more strongly identified with our cause—and I'm referring not to how much we *care* about the cause but to how much we derive our sense of identity from it—are more likely to have an ingrouping mentality.

Ingrouping has obvious consequences for how we relate to those outside our cause. If we see the very people we need to attract as inferior, our outreach is unlikely to be as effective as it could be. But ingrouping also has consequences for how we relate to advocates within our movement. Much infighting is caused by advocates who've created an ingroup within their group. These advocates espouse the belief that their particular approach to challenging oppression is superior, and they disrespect and bully those who don't agree with them.

Post-Traumatic Stress

Perhaps the most significant consequence of advocates' awareness of injustices is the traumatization they can experience as a result of that awareness. In previous chapters, we discussed such traumatization, as well as its accompanying trauma narrative (the worldview we develop in which we place everyone into one of three rigid categories—perpetrator, victim, or hero).

Post-traumatic stress contributes to infighting in a variety of ways. For example, as we've discussed, traumatization can cause us to become dysregulated: our anger and grief—which are normal and healthy responses to witnessing injustice—can intensify to the point where we're unable to manage them. We can end up feeling highly sensitized to even the slightest of stressors, such as misunderstandings or perceived affronts, reacting defensively and causing the person on the receiving end of our reaction to feel dysregulated and defensive as well. In other words, the emotional dysregulation that accompanies trauma can cause us to engage in nonrelational behaviors that then dysregulate, or further dysregulate, others in the movement. As long as we're not regulated enough, we're unlikely to relate to one another (or to those outside our movement) in a way that's healthy. In addition, our dysregulation increases our risk of becoming further traumatized, because it makes us more self-neglecting and disconnected from the relational connections that are necessary for resilience and healing.

Post-traumatic stress can also increase the tendency to ingroup. The trauma narrative, along with our survivor guilt, can exacerbate our sense of moral superiority and rigid either-or, us-versus-them thinking. When we think of others and ourselves as being either "all good" or "all bad," and we feel guilty for not being "good enough"—for not doing enough to end injustice—we can look for scapegoats to offset our guilt. We look for people to blame for the problem and for our distressing emotions.

Scapegoating is a common consequence of ingrouping. Often, the scapegoats we create are people outside the movement, people who are enabling the injustice by, for instance, voting for politicians who wage unjust wars or who promote oppressive anti-immigration legislation. Of course, people who support injustice *are* in part responsible for the problem. However, when we scapegoat, we're not simply recognizing that these people's behaviors are problematic; we're using them as a means to manage our own emotions. Scapegoating can also cause us to blame people who aren't, in fact, blameworthy—or, for those who *are* part of the problem, to exaggerate how much they are responsible for it.

Sometimes we create scapegoats within our movement. For example, advocates who feel guilty for not doing enough for the cause or feel frustrated by their sense of helplessness to end the injustice may attack other advocates in an attempt to avoid and offset their personal discomfort.

Post-traumatic stress can also cause us to become perfectionistic. The trauma narrative can drive us to feel like we, and others, can and should live up to an impossible ideal. We start to believe that if we're not heroes, living perfectly in alignment with our moral values all the time, and we're not victims, then we must be perpetrators. In order not to have to think of ourselves as perpetrators, we can end up striving to avoid doing or saying anything that isn't ideal or perfect.

Perfectionism
Perfectionism is the belief that individuals and things (e.g., events, activities) can and should be perfect. But since everything can

be improved upon indefinitely, perfection is an impossible goal. Perfectionism is a belief based on an illusion.

Perfectionism is a major obstacle to achieving any goal, and, not surprisingly, it fuels infighting. Infighting, in turn, drives perfectionism. For example, when we believe that advocates have to be perfect, we're more likely to be rigid in our thinking and to feel contemptuous of others and ashamed of ourselves. We're also more likely to get frustrated with others or ourselves when they or we aren't perfect, feeding our collective dysregulation. Frustration is the feeling that results from things not being the way we think they should be—from our expectations not being met. Our frustration is always commensurate with our expectations. So when we expect perfection and don't get it, we feel frustrated. We also feel judgmental, since we perceive anything less than perfect as flawed, or even as a failure.

When we feel we can and should be perfect, we can avoid doing important things, such as trying new outreach methods or sharing our opinions or strategic insights. We're worried that when we make mistakes (which we will, as everyone does), we'll see ourselves and be seen by others as having failed. We may also waste precious time trying to perfect our campaigns and activities rather than accepting them as good enough and moving on to new ones. Perfectionism prevents us from thinking creatively and acting effectively; people who fear making mistakes are often those who end up doing nothing. Learning to "fail well"—learning and growing from our mistakes—is essential to our being able to achieve our goals.

Many advocates fear and resist appearing imperfect because the dominant culture projects the expectation of perfection on us. As we discussed in Chapter 5, we often get the message that we have to be perfect ambassadors for our cause if we hope to advocate effectively. For instance, if we lose our temper during a heated conversation about injustice, we're framed as the unhinged, angry activist; and if we admit that we don't have all the answers to the problem our movement is trying to solve, as noted, someone will use this as an excuse to invalidate everything we stand for. When we buy into these projections, we can cling more tightly to perfectionistic thinking.

The all-or-nothing attitude inherent in perfectionism can also scare off many potential new supporters of our movement. When people see that there are only two ways to approach an issue—you're either part of the solution or part of the problem—and they're unable or unwilling to get fully on board with what we're stating the solution is, we leave them with no other options to help transform a problematic, nonrelational system. As the renowned animal rights activist Henry Spira pointed out, when we go into a negotiation asking for all or nothing, we usually end up with nothing.

The belief that someone is either part of the solution or part of the problem makes intuitive sense. It's easy to understand why people would think this way. However, this belief is both inaccurate and counterproductive. People can and do occupy multiple roles within a given system; we're all, in some ways, both part of the problem and part of the solution. The world we live in is messy and imperfect, and we have to make choices that, in an ideal world, we wouldn't be faced with. It's not possible to live in perfect alignment with our highest values in a world so steeped in dysfunction.

When we step out of the perfectionistic mindset, we can see how people can be, and often are, both supporters and detractors of a cause. Consider, for example, nonvegans who eat animals but who donate money to vegan organizations or write articles or produce films raising awareness of carnism. Many of these nonvegans end up helping far more animals than they harm with their diet, resulting in a net-positive impact on the movement. And consider vegans who don't eat animals but represent the movement so ineffectively that they probably have a net-negative impact, causing more harm than they offset. By saying things like, "You can't throw money at [donate to] an issue if you don't live within those values," they're communicating that if someone isn't vegan, they shouldn't be doing anything to help animals. This is like telling a nonvegan who's willing to jump in the water to save a drowning piglet not to bother.

Embrace Imperfection

It's important to recognize perfectionism for what it is and to appreciate that we have no choice but to live with contradictions and make imperfect choices because we've inherited an imperfect world.

In general, advocates for justice are visionaries. We have a vision of how the world *could* be, which, in our minds, easily translates to how the world *should* be. But we need to relate to the world as it is rather than as we wish it were. Doing so will save us a tremendous amount of stress and frustration.

When we give others and ourselves permission to be the messy, complicated, fallible people we all are, we give a great gift. Our relationships with those who share our values and those who don't—and our relationship with ourselves—will likely improve immensely. And we help reduce infighting and build the resilience of our movement.

In *Think Again*, Adam Grant explains how organizations in which imperfection is embraced are more resilient and effective. Such organizations are highly innovative, and their staff make the fewest harmful mistakes. This is because people feel psychologically safe and they are therefore willing to take risks, knowing they won't be punished for doing so. They also trust others, such that they feel comfortable admitting to having made mistakes (and they trust that others will admit to having made mistakes), so any mishaps that do occur get sorted out. When people fear making mistakes, not only do they not have the opportunity to learn from them, but they are also more likely to cover up errors, which then never get resolved and can lead to major problems. Mistakes need to be made so that people can learn and grow and succeed. And when we relate to mistakes in a healthy way, they can benefit rather than harm us, our organization, and our movement.

Our Default Change Strategy Is Counterproductive

Another key reason for infighting is that the change strategy many of us tend to default to is counterproductive.[4] This change strategy is based on a set of longstanding and widespread assumptions about the best ways to get others to change their attitudes and behaviors. It's often referred to as the "confrontational" approach; however, it has been more accurately described as the "*aggressive* confrontational" approach because its methods are based on force, both subtle and overt.

This strategy began as an intervention to treat addiction in the US in the mid-twentieth century, before eventually spreading to the field of psychotherapy and then trickling into the mainstream. The questions for those trying to treat addiction were: How does one inspire change in someone else? What methods or interventions do we need to use to get someone to stop engaging in a behavior that's causing harm to themself and others?

Those asking these questions were not psychologists but laypeople who were trying to manage their own addictions— members of voluntary, peer-based communities that were comprised mostly of white men.[5] And the answers they came up with were highly subjective, as there were no established protocols for reliably evaluating the effectiveness of such treatments.

The belief was that people who suffered from addiction needed to be "broken down" in order to be "built back up." Psychotherapists who later became involved in treatment interventions hypothesized that "addicts" suffered from a defective personality that caused them to be so defensive that only direct, aggressive verbal confrontations (such as forcing them to confess that they were weak, inept, selfish, and so on) would reach them. The belief was that if people could be made to feel bad enough about their behaviors, they'd want to change them.

Once empirical research on these treatments was conducted, the aggressive confrontational approach was shown to be not only ineffective but counterproductive. It turns out that such confrontation doesn't break through defensiveness; it *causes* it— and, as such, reduces the chances that the person being confronted will be receptive to requests for change.

Unfortunately, however, many of us—especially in our roles as advocates—have bought into the belief that confronting others in such a manner about what we see as their problematic attitudes and behaviors is appropriate and effective. Even when the pressure we exert is subtle, as when we cause the other person to feel guilty about or ashamed of their way of thinking or behaving, this approach tends to bring about outcomes that are the opposite of what we want.

Confrontation Fuels Infighting

The aggressive confrontational approach fuels infighting for a variety of reasons and in myriad ways. Most notably, this approach causes us to try to influence other advocates by using shaming and other nonrelational behaviors, leading to mutual defensiveness and reducing our sense of security and connection with one another. It causes us to relate to our differences as battles, preventing us from having the open discussions necessary for creative problem-solving. And it causes us to become increasingly wedded to our own opinions and, as a result, increasingly siloed.

Alternatives to Confrontation

What the research shows is that the most effective way to elicit change in others—both those within our movement and those outside it—is not through aggression but through compassion. People are more likely to change not through force but through encouragement. Rather than try to shame someone into changing or persuade them to change, we motivate them to *want* to change.

A large body of research has found that the most effective change strategy is *motivational interviewing*. Motivational interviewing is discussing an issue in a way such that the other person will feel intrinsically motivated to change; it is helping them see the value in changing so that they desire change.[6]

In fact, studies have shown that simply listening to someone—with empathy and without judgment—leads to that person developing more clarity about their own attitudes, with less rigidity around and attachment to those attitudes. Research also shows that when people are asked to reflect on the nuances in their thinking, their views become more open and less extreme. Studies have shown as well that when we reflect back to someone how arbitrary their beliefs are—how sexist or carnistic attitudes, for instance, are essentially an accident of birth—they are more likely to reconsider such attitudes.[7] For example, we might point out that if a man had been born into a woman's body, or if a European had been born into a culture where people eat dogs, then their attitudes toward women and eating animals, respectively, would be dramatically different.

Research on persuasion techniques supports these findings. As Adam Grant explains, "Preaching and prosecuting typically backfire—and what doesn't sway people may strengthen their beliefs. Much as a vaccine inoculates the physical immune system against a virus, the act of resistance fortifies the psychological immune system. Refuting a point of view produces antibodies against future attempts at influence, making people more certain of their own opinions and more ready to rebut alternatives."[8]

When we communicate relationally and know how to ask the kinds of questions that help motivate others to self-reflect, our efforts to encourage them toward change are much more likely to be effective.

Preventing Infighting Superspreader Events

Because infighting reflects and reinforces relational dysfunction, it tends to reproduce itself, to be contagious. And many attacks by advocates on other advocates occur online. The nonrelational communication gets funneled through the digital megaphone that is social media to create a sort of superspreader event, affecting countless advocates at a time, and turning off many potential supporters to their cause in the process. Studies have shown that people can and do catch emotions through social media posts, emails, and other digital modes of transmission.[9]

In fact, social media is structured to prevent relational communication and accurate information, and to encourage the opposite. It is also structured to dysregulate us and to cause our thinking to become increasingly shallow. What this means is that if we hope to mitigate infighting, we need to be vigilant about not supporting or spreading communications that berate or otherwise shame others in our movement. We need to avoid allowing such posts to live on our pages or helping them get upvotes.

Remembering Our Shared Mission

Often, when we feel critical of another advocate, we forget that we share the same goal, that we're working toward the same mission. It's easy to forget that the other advocate is a person who, in all likelihood, cares very much about the cause and doesn't want to enable harm. In the same vein, we often forget that the organization we may want to criticize is made up of people who also care a great deal about their contributions to the cause.

So before communicating to or about another advocate or organization, assume goodwill. Assume that the person who said or did something you disagree with, or the organization that framed its message in a way you found offensive, nevertheless felt that that was the right thing to do to further the cause for justice. Pause and ask yourself if there might be a good reason for a given behavior that you see as problematic—not as an excuse, but as an explanation for it. Give others the benefit of the doubt.

Ending Injustice Everywhere

Martin Luther King, Jr. famously said that injustice anywhere is a threat to justice everywhere. This statement makes intuitive sense. And when we understand the contagious nature of unjust, nonrelational behaviors, we can truly appreciate how injustice reproduces itself, no matter where it shows up, no matter from or to whom it's directed.

That injustice breeds injustice is why it's so important that those of us who want to create a better world recognize the nonrelational common denominator driving all injustices. Every time we choose integrity over indignation, compassion over contempt, dignity over defensiveness—every time we avert an unjust dynamic and practice a just one instead—we're interrupting the process of nonrelational dysfunction that's at the root of so much suffering and harm, and we're redirecting that process toward healing. Even if we've already said or done something that's caused harm, even if we're in the middle of a power struggle, we can still course-correct by reaching out to offer repair or by pivoting mid-interaction to practice the formula for healthy relating. In this way, the Golden Rule shifts from being an impossible ideal that's regularly violated to a practical reality that's consistently honored. As Desmond Tutu said, "We are each made for goodness, love and compassion. Our lives are transformed as much as the world is when we live with these truths."[10] In other words, our minute-to-minute lives come to serve a broader mission of justice, as they become platforms for relational transformation.

And the tools for transformation lie within us. Research has shown that we are hardwired to empathize with others,[11] so in many ways, empathy is our natural state. We therefore don't have to learn how to care as much as unlearn how not to care. We simply need to more fully access our authentic selves—to reconnect with the parts of ourselves that have been buried beneath the fear, anger, and shame of nonrelational conditioning.

When we bring such awareness and authenticity to our movements for justice, they, too, can be transformed. Once we're aware of the common denominator driving all injustices, we can appreciate that no matter what our specific mission may be—justice for humans, animals, or the environment—it's part of a broader, shared metamission: to create a more relational world.

Working toward this metamission doesn't mean we have to take resources away from our more targeted individual missions. Obviously, we have only so much time, energy, focus, and interest to dedicate to our advocacy, and we need to choose which cause(s) we want to directly support. But we can nevertheless maintain a commitment to practicing unconditional relationality by, at the very least, not harming other movements as we work to fulfill the mission of our own. For example, we can choose not to demean nonhuman beings in order to dignify human beings—not saying, for instance, that a particular human group "doesn't deserve to be treated like animals"—just as we can (and must) not demean human beings when we advocate justice for other animals. Ideally, we wouldn't simply avoid harming other movements but would actively work to support them—through our messaging, networking, collaborations, and so on.

When we appreciate the metamission, our advocacy work becomes less like a no-win game of Whac-A-Mole and more like an all-win alliance for global justice. Rather than target one injustice at a time, we address the deeper processes that drive all injustices. Rather than use the same dysfunctional method that keeps causing new injustices to pop up, we lay down the mallet.

Indeed, not only is injustice anywhere a threat to justice everywhere, but justice anywhere is a threat to injustice everywhere. And never before has the success of our justice movements been more urgent. As unjust systems have been left largely unchecked, they've grown into global tyrannies that are driving global catastrophes: brutal wars, fascist regimes, mass poverty, ubiquitous pandemics, unspeakable animal exploitation, and imminent ecological collapse. And these systems all intersect with and reinforce one another, creating a global system of injustice that is greater than the sum of its parts.

But when we unite behind our shared metamission, our movements, too, can become mutually reinforcing. We can create a unified global movement for justice that is greater than the sum of its parts. Together, we can pose the most formidable challenge to injustice and carry the most powerful beacon of hope.

NOTES

Preface

1. The perspective I bring to this book inevitably reflects those of the various groups—groups that are privileged and groups that are harmed by others' privilege—to which I belong. I understand that as a white, able-bodied, cisgender woman, I cannot fully appreciate the experiences of members of the groups of which I am not a member.

2. Many philosophers have explored how to determine whether an individual is deserving of moral consideration, asking: What should be the defining criterion? Most philosophers today agree that all human beings deserve moral consideration—though such consideration may be forfeited through one's subsequent actions or inactions. A more controversial question has been whether nonhuman animals should be included in the sphere of moral consideration. Peter Singer suggests that the defining criterion for moral consideration is *sentience*, the capacity to feel pleasure and pain. And because nonhuman animals, like human animals, are sentient—that is, they have feelings and are vulnerable to harm—they deserve moral consideration. Tom Regan suggests that the criterion for moral consideration is being a "subject of a life," which entails having self-consciousness, emotions, and certain types of cognitive processes. Thus, Regan also argues that nonhuman animals must be included in the sphere of moral consideration. For more information on this issue, see Singer, Peter. *Animal Liberation: A New Ethics for*

Our Treatment of Animals. New York: New York Review, 1975; and Regan, Tom. *The Case for Animal Rights.* Berkeley: University of California Press, 2004. First published 1983.

3. I am aware that the term "animal" is speciesist, as it categorizes humans as separate from all other animals. However, I've chosen to use this term at times to avoid language that detracts from the clarity or flow of the text.

4. It has been argued that the ecosystems that are homes for nonhuman animals and that comprise living flora should also be included in the sphere of moral consideration. By including this point, I am not suggesting that plants and animals have the same interests, but that the interests of ecosystems warrant consideration. Our current course of ecological devastation reflects precisely what happens when we don't consider those interests.

5. A small sample includes such seminal works as: Freire, Paulo. *Pedagogy of the Oppressed.* New York: Continuum, 2000. First published 1970; Fanon, Frantz. *The Wretched of the Earth.* New York: Grove Press, 1963; hooks, bell. *Ain't I a Woman: Black Women and Feminism.* New York: Routledge, 2015. First published 1981; Lifton, Jay. *The Genocidal Mentality: Nazi Holocaust and Nuclear Threat.* London: Macmillan, 1991; and, more recently, Alexander, Michelle. *The New Jim Crow: Mass Incarceration in the Age of Colorblindness.* New York: New Press, 2011.

Chapter 1

1. See, for example, Polish, Jennifer. "Decolonizing Veganism: On Resisting Vegan Whiteness and Racism." In *Critical Perspectives on Veganism*, edited by Jodey Castricano and Rasmus R. Simonsen, 373–91. Palgrave Macmillan Animal Ethics Series. London: Palgrave Macmillan, 2016. doi:10.1007/978-3-319-33419-6_17; Harper, Breeze. *Sistah Vegan: Black Female Vegans Speak on Food, Identity, Health, and Society.* New York: Lantern, 2009; McQuirter, Tracye Lynn. *By Any Greens Necessary: A Revolutionary Guide for Black Women Who Want to Eat Great, Get Healthy, Lose Weight, and Look Phat.* Chicago: Chicago Review Press, 2010.

2. The same relational dynamics that enable oppression—the unjust use of power in a system in which there is an inequality of power and privilege between social groups—also enable abuse, which is the unjust use of power that is wielded against those who are not (necessarily) members of disenfranchised groups and that is often carried out on the interpersonal (or sometimes intrapersonal) level. This point is discussed further in Chapter 2.

3. I acknowledge that oppression is a social, external phenomenon; however, I believe that if we wish to transform oppression, we need to recognize how oppressive dynamics are also carried out in the other relational dimensions.

4. There is a growing body of research on relationality (see, for example, the work of John Gottman and Julie Schwartz Gottman at https://www.gottman.com/). However, for our purposes, perhaps the most notable research comes from the field of relational-cultural theory (RCT). RCT holds that relationships lie at the core of individual and social functioning and that healthy relationships, which comprise healthy relational behaviors, are essential for individual and social wellbeing. In this book, I draw on the work that informs RCT (developed in large part by Jean Baker Miller, Judith V. Jordan, Janet Surrey, and Irene Stiver from the Wellesley College Stone Center), expanding that theory to include relationships beyond those between and among humans, and suggesting a model and structure with which to understand all nonrelational systems. (See Miller, Jean Baker, and Irene Pierce Stiver. *The Healing Connection: How Women Form Relationships in Therapy and in Life.* Boston: Beacon Press, 1997; Surrey, Janet L. "Relationship and Empowerment." In *Women's Growth in Connection: Writings from the Stone Center*, edited by Judith V. Jordan, Alexandra G. Kaplan, Irene P. Stiver, Janet L. Surrey, and Jean Baker Miller. New York: Guilford Press, 1991; and West, Carolyn K. "The Map of Relational Cultural Theory." *Women & Therapy* 28, no. 3–4 (2005): 93–110, doi:10.1300/J015v28n03_05.) Other significant research on relationality comes from attachment theory, which holds that the way we attach to others is central to how we view and behave toward others and

ourselves. See Ainsworth, Mary D. Salter. "Attachments and Other Affectional Bonds across the Life Cycle." In *Attachment across the Life Cycle*, edited by Colin Murray Parkes, Joan Stevenson-Hinde, and Peter Marris, 33–51. London: Routledge, 1991; Bowlby, John. *Attachment and Loss*. Vol. 1, *Attachment*, 2nd ed. New York: Basic Books, 1982. First published 1969.

5. The formula I propose is based on my analysis following a comprehensive review of the literature on healthy relationality and on my own experience working in the relationship space.

6. I am including in the collective dimension how we relate to nonhuman animals and the environment.

7. For an examination of our relationship with and responsibilities to nonhuman animals, see *Justice for Animals: Our Collective Responsibility*, by Martha C. Nussbaum and *Animal Liberation*, by Peter Singer.

8. The most comprehensive research on moral values was conducted by Jonathan Haidt and Jesse Grahm, which served as the basis of their moral foundations theory. Haidt and Grahm found that five moral values are shared across cultures and that two of those values— caring and fairness (compassion and justice)—are most equitably espoused by all individuals. For more on moral foundations theory, see moralfoundations.org and Haidt, Jonathan. *The Righteous Mind: Why Good People Are Divided by Politics and Religion*. New York: Pantheon Books, 2012.

9. I am aware that some of the key relational constructs I refer to, such as power and shame, reflect a Western view of relationships and that more research is needed examining how such constructs are understood and experienced cross-culturally. However, some research suggests considerable consistency in how these phenomena are experienced across cultures. See, for example, Sznycer, Daniel, John Tooby, Leda Cosmides, Roni Porat, Shaul Shalvi, and Eran Halperin. "Shame Closely Tracks the Threat of Devaluation by Others, Even across Cultures." *Proceedings of the National Academy of Sciences* 113, no. 10 (2016): 2625–30.

Chapter 2

1. For an interesting introductory read on contemporary casteism, see "With Stories of Her Oppressed Community, a Journalist Takes Aim at the Walls of Caste" by Karan Deep Singh. *New York Times*, March 6, 2023. https://www.nytimes.com/2023/03/06/world/asia/india-caste-discrimination-dalit-journalist-mooknayak.html.

2. The same dynamics that underlie oppressive behaviors toward others also underlie self-destructive behaviors.

3. Associated Press. "U.S. Court Rules Jews Are Protected 'Race' under Civil Rights Act of 1964." *Haaretz*, July 19, 2018. https://www.haaretz.com/us-news/u-s-court-rules-jews-are-protected-race-under-civil-rights-act-1.6291921. See also US Senate Committee of Health, Education, Labor and Pensions. Anti-Semitism Awareness Act of 2018. S. 2940, 11th Cong., 2nd sess. https://www.congress.gov/115/bills/s2940/BILLS-115s2940is.xml.

4. White House. Protecting the Nation from Foreign Terrorist Entry into the United States. Executive order 13780 (January 27, 2017). *Federal Register* 82, no. 20 (February 15, 2017): 8977–82. https://www.dhs.gov/publication/executive-order-13780-protecting-nation-foreign-terrorist-entry-united-states-initial#:~:text=Trump%20issued%20Executive%20Order%2013780,of%20actions%20to%20enhance%20the. See also *Supreme Court of the United States: Trump, President of the United States, et al. v. Hawaii et al.* (No. 17-965, June 26, 2018). https://www.supremecourt.gov/opinions/17pdf/17-965_h315.pdf.

5. Carson, E. Ann. *Prisoners in 2016.* Bureau of Justice Statistics, US Department of Justice, Office of Justice Programs. August 7, 2018. https://www.bjs.gov/content/pub/pdf/p16.pdf. See also Alexander, Michelle. *The New Jim Crow: Mass Incarceration in the Age of Colorblindness.* New York: New Press, 2011; and Duvernay, Ava (director). *13th.* 2016. Netflix. https://www.netflix.com/de/title/80091741.

6. For an excellent examination of capitalism and climate change see Klein, Naomi, *This Changes Everything: Capitalism vs. the Climate.* New York: Simon and Schuster, 2015.

7.   Some scholars suggest that racism is the foundation of some other forms of oppression. See, for example, Ko, Aph, and Syl Ko. *Aphroism: Essays on Pop Culture, Feminism, and Black Veganism from Two Sisters*. New York: Lantern Books, 2017.

8.   Kimberlé Crenshaw has done vitally important work illuminating how oppressions intersect and what this means for social justice. See Crenshaw, Kimberlé. "Demarginalizing the Intersection of Race and Sex: A Black Feminist Critique of Antidiscrimination Doctrine, Feminist Theory and Antiracist Politics." *University of Chicago Legal Forum*, no. 1 (1989): art. 8. http://chicagounbound.uchicago.edu/uclf/vol1989/iss1/8.

9.   Also see the work of Angela Davis for excellent analyses of intersecting oppressions.

10. Tasca, Cecilia, Mariangela Rapetti, Mauro Giovanni Carta, and Bianca Fadda. "Women and Hysteria in the History of Mental Health." *Clinical Practice and Epidemiology in Mental Health* 8 (2012): 110–19.

11. I have, as much as possible, avoided using terms that reflect gender binarism. I have used such terms only when they've been necessary to accurately communicate a concept. To this end, I have also chosen to use the singular pronoun *they*.

12. Hicks, Donna. *Dignity: The Essential Role It Plays in Resolving Conflict*. New Haven, CT: Yale University Press, 2011.

13. Joy, Melanie. "Compassion Privilege: Why Kind People Close Their Hearts." *Psychology Today*. April 13, 2021. https://www.psychologytoday.com/us/blog/relational-literacy/202104/compassion-privilege-why-kind-people-close-their-hearts.

14. See, for example, David, E.J.R., and Annie O. Derthick. *The Psychology of Oppression*. New York: Springer, 2017; Guinote, Ana, and Theresa K. Vescio, eds. *The Social Psychology of Power*. New York: Guilford Press, 2010; Prilleltensky, Isaac, and Dennis R. Fox. "Psychopolitical Literacy for Wellness and Justice." *Journal of Community Psychology* 35, no. 6 (2007): 793–805; Oliver, Kelly. *The Colonization of Psychic Space: A Psychoanalytic Social Theory of Oppression*. Minneapolis: University of Minnesota Press, 2004; Miller, Jean Baker. *Toward a New Psychology of*

Women. Boston: Beacon Press, 1987. First published 1976; and Fanon, Frantz. *The Wretched of the Earth.* New York: Grove Press, 1963.

15. Hicks, *Dignity.*

16. This trend is fortunately changing. Some notable works examining the role of psychology in enabling oppression include David and Derthick, *Psychology of Oppression*; Ratner, Carl. *Macro Cultural Psychology: A Political Philosophy of Mind.* New York: Oxford University Press, 2012; Guinote and Vescio, *Social Psychology of Power*; Fox, Dennis, Isaac Prilleltensky, and Stephanie Austin, eds. *Critical Psychology: An Introduction*, 2nd ed. Thousand Oaks, CA: Sage, 2009; Oliver, *Colonization of Psychic Space*; Miller, *Toward a New Psychology of Women*; Fanon, *Wretched of the Earth*; and Fromm, Erich. *The Pathology of Normalcy.* New York: American Mental Health Foundation Books, 2010. First published 1953.

17. See, for example, Banks, Amy, and Leigh Ann Hirschman. *Wired to Connect: The Surprising Link between Brain Science and Strong, Healthy Relationships.* New York: TarcherPerigee, 2016; Jordan, Judith V., ed. *The Power of Connection: Recent Developments in Relational-Cultural Theory.* New York: Routledge, 2010; and Tatkin, Stan. *Wired for Love: How Understanding Your Partner's Brain and Attachment Style Can Help You Defuse Conflict and Build a Secure Relationship.* Oakland, CA: New Harbinger, 2012.

18. For an excellent overview of attachment styles and how they impact relational dynamics, see Levine, Amir, and Rachel S. F. Heller. *Attached: The New Science of Adult Attachment and How It Can Help You Find—and Keep—Love.* New York: TarcherPerigee, 2010.

19. See Ainsworth, "Attachments."

20. Research on the influence of systems on attachment styles could yield important information regarding what kinds of political, economic, and other institutions promote or hinder social wellbeing.

21. Sometimes people in a relationship start out with equal amounts of power, but the abusive dynamic creates an imbalance.

22. See Bancroft, Lundy. *Why Does He Do That? Inside the Minds of Angry and Controlling Men.* New York: Berkeley Books, 2002.

23. For a history of the role of institutionalized patriarchy in normalizing domestic violence, see Dobash, R. Emerson, and Russell Dobash. *Violence against Wives: A Case against the Patriarchy*. New York: Free Press, 1979. For a more recent discussion of the use of patriarchy as a model for understanding domestic violence, see Hunnicutt, Gwen. "Varieties of Patriarchy and Violence against Women: Resurrecting 'Patriarchy' as a Theoretical Tool." *Violence against Women* 15, no. 5 (2009): 553–73. https://doi.org/10.1177/1077801208331246.

Chapter 3

1. This statement is frequently attributed to both Adolf Hitler and Joseph Goebbels. It appears to derive from Hitler's discussion, in *Mein Kampf*, of a propaganda technique he associates with Jews and Marxists.

2. This quote appears in print in the screenplay of *Gandhi* (1982) by John Briley. Briley, John. *Gandhi: The Screenplay*. London: Duckworth, 1982. This quote has been widely attributed to Gandhi but there is some question as to its original source. The passage subsequently appears in Ronald Reagan's address to the United Nations General Assembly on September 24, 1984. See "Transcript of Reagan's Address to the U.N. General Assembly." *New York Times Archives,* September 25, 1984. https://www.nytimes.com/1984/09/25/world/transcript-of-reagan-s-address-to-the-un-general-assembly.html?pagewanted=all.

3. For a detailed discussion of various forms of power, see Guinote, Ana, and Theresa K. Vescio, eds. *The Social Psychology of Power.* New York: Guilford Press, 2010.

4. I use *powerful* in the technical sense of the term, to denote either being or feeling "full" of power—having or believing one has the ability to act or influence. I also use *powerful* (as a feeling) to describe the "high" that has been shown to correlate with this feeling, which reflects an increase in dopamine and as such has led some researchers to suggest that power is addictive. (I am operating under the assumption that feeling powerful exists on a spectrum, and that the corresponding high emerges when one has a sufficient level of this feeling.) So feeling

"powerful" can mean feeling one has the power to act or influence and/or feeling high from having a certain amount of power.

5. I use *empowered* and *feeling empowered* to denote having the ability to act or influence and the feeling one has when they have this ability, respectively. Although *powerful* and *empowered* are synonymous in one sense (having or believing that one has the ability to act or influence), there are two differences in how these terms may be interpreted. First, feeling powerful is often (though not always) a comparative experience, meaning that one may feel more or less powerful based on how their level of power compares to that of another, whereas one tends to feel empowered (or not) regardless of whether or not others are empowered. Second, although the feeling of being powerful has been shown to correlate with an increase in dopamine, it appears that no similar studies have been done on the neurochemistry of empowerment, and I am operating under the assumption that feeling empowered does not entail feeling a high.

6. For a comprehensive discussion of self-perception and psychosocial functioning, see Bandura, Albert. *Self-Efficacy: The Exercise of Self-Control.* New York: W.H. Freedman and Company, 1997.

7. The process of an interaction often reflects the purpose. For instance, when we abuse rather than respect power, the way we use power (the process) in this instance reflects our wish to harm or control another (the purpose). Sometimes, however, the process and the purpose differ. For example, perhaps we abuse power not in order to negatively impact another or others but because we don't care about our impact on them, as when we purchase a high-emissions vehicle that we know causes damage to the environment. Or, in certain cases, we're simply not aware that we're abusing power. Regardless of our motivation, the process we use can cause harm, and it is primarily on the level of process that nonrelational systems are maintained or transformed.

8. One of the most notable researchers examining the intersection of power, prejudice, social cognition, and stereotypes is Susan Fiske. See, for example, Fiske, S. T. "Controlling Other People: The Impact of Power on Stereotyping." *American Psychologist* 48, no. 6 (1993): 621– 28. http://dx.doi.org/10.1037/0003-066X.48.6.621.

9. I don't mean to oversimplify the complex issue of power models and power dynamics. I don't provide a more nuanced analysis because the purpose of this book is not to examine the intricacies of power structures but to give an overview of power models simply as they relate to relationality.

10. I use *disempowerment* to denote either the state or the feeling of lacking the agency to act or influence. In other words, a person can *be* disempowered (lacking agency) or can *feel* disempowered (lacking belief in the agency that they actually have).

11. Breakthrough studies in neuroscience have shown that we are actually hardwired for connection—that we are fundamentally relational beings who strive for connection and seek to avoid the pain of disconnection just as we seek to avoid physical pain. Data also shows that the brain grows in connection. See, for example, Gerhardt, Sue. *Why Love Matters: How Affection Shapes a Baby's Brain.* Hove, East Sussex, UK: Brunner-Routledge, 2004.

12. For more information on the functionalist model, see Overbeck, Jennifer R. "Concepts and Historical Perspectives on Power." In *The Social Psychology of Power*, edited by Guinote and Vescio, 19–45.

13. The power models I describe here are based on the dominance and functionalist models noted in the social science literature, and they include the concepts provided by Mary Parker Follett, who coined the terms *power over* and *power with* to describe distinct models of power. They also borrow from the conceptual model of Kenneth Boulding, who built on Follett's analysis and described "threat," "exchange," and "love" as forms of power, and that of Jean Baker Miller, who put forth a relational model of power. I have slightly modified the functionalist/power with model to reflect a synthesis and extended analysis of the corresponding theories. See Follet, Mary P. *Dynamic Administration: The Collected Papers of Mary Parker Follet,* edited by E. M. Fox and L. Urwick. London: Pitman Publishing, 1940; Boulding, Kenneth E. *Three Faces of Power.* Newbury Park, CA: Sage Publications, 1989; and Miller, Jean B. *Toward a New Psychology of Women.* Boston: Beacon Press, 1987.

14. Tracy, Jessica L., and Robins, Richard W. "Death of a (Narcissistic) Salesman: An Integrative Model of Fragile Self-Esteem: Comment." *Psychological Inquiry* 14, no. 1 (2003): 57–62.

15. Although culture plays a significant role in determining what qualities we define as affording one power, individual subjectivity also plays a role. For example, even if we live in a culture that largely conflates beauty and power, we may not personally hold beauty in such high regard. So, even though we are still heavily influenced by the broader culture, we may nevertheless afford beauty less status compared to someone whose personal values coincide more fully with those of the culture.

16. For an insightful reflection on otherness as a basis for subjugation, see Morrison, Toni. *The Origin of Others.* Cambridge, MA: Harvard University Press, 2017.

17. Sometimes, the only thing someone can influence (or try to influence) is how they relate to the circumstances in which they find themself.

18. Shafer, Carolyn M., and Marilyn Frye. "Rape and Respect." In *Feminism and Philosophy*, edited by Mary Vetterling-Braggin, Frederick A. Elliston, and Jane English, 333–46. Savage, MD: Rowman & Littlefield, 1977.

19. Bloom, Sandra L., and Brian Farragher. "Authoritarianism, Learned Helplessness, and Disempowerment." In *Destroying Sanctuary: The Crisis in Human Service Delivery Systems.* New York: Oxford University Press, 2011; Young, Judith H. "Psychological Control: States of Mental Disempowerment." *Global Research*, October 25, 2008. https://www.globalresearch.ca/psychological-control-states-of-mental-disempowerment/10687.

20. Singer, Margaret T. "Therapy with Ex-Cult Members." *Journal of the National Association of Private Psychiatric Hospitals* 9, no. 4 (1978): 14–18; Clark, John G., Jr. "Cults." *Journal of the American Medical Association* 242, no. 3 (1979): 279–81. doi:10.1001/jama.1979.033 00030051026.

21. Carballo, David M., Paul Roscoe, and Gary M. Feinman. "Cooperation and Collective Action in the Cultural Evolution of Complex Societies." *Journal of Archaeological Method and Theory* 21, no. 1 (March 2014): 98–133.

22. When I refer to empowerment throughout this book, I am referring to "relational" empowerment—the empowerment of individuals to act in relationally healthful ways.

23. Strohminger, Nina, and Shaun Nichols. "The Essential Moral Self." *Cognition—International Journal of Cognitive Science* 131, no. 1 (2014): 159–71.

24. Peck, M. Scott. *The Road Less Traveled: A New Psychology of Love, Traditional Values, and Spiritual Growth.* New York: Simon & Schuster, 1978.

25. See Tolle, Eckhart. *The Power of Now: A Guide to Spiritual Enlightenment.* Novato, CA: New World Library, 1999.

26. See Scheff, Thomas J., and Suzanne M. Retzinger. *Emotions and Violence: Shame and Rage in Destructive Conflicts.* Self-published, iUniverse, 2001; and Hicks, Donna. *Dignity: The Essential Role It Plays in Resolving Conflict.* New Haven, CT: Yale University Press, 2011.

27. Of course, in and of themselves, these behaviors don't necessarily mean we are compensating for shame; the determining factor is our motivation for engaging in such behaviors.

28. See Hicks, *Dignity.*

29. Lickel, Brian, Kostadin Kushlev, Victoria Savalei, Shashi Matta, and Toni Schmader. "Shame and the Motivation to Change the Self." *Emotion* 14, no. 6 (2014): 1049–61; Iyer, Aarti, Toni Schmader, and Brian Lickel. "Why Individuals Protest the Perceived Transgressions of Their Country: The Role of Anger, Shame, and Guilt." *Personality and Social Psychology Bulletin* 33, no. 4 (2007): 572–87.

30. Jacquet, Jennifer. *Is Shame Necessary? New Uses for an Old Tool.* New York: Vintage, 2015; O'Neil, Cathy. *The Shame Machine: Who Profits in the New Age of Humiliation.* New York: Crown, 2022.

31. Different individuals respond to traumatizing events in different ways; here, I describe the common denominators that cause traumatization in most people.

32. There are a variety of reasons for trauma being so disconnecting; for an excellent resource, see Herman, Judith. *Trauma and Recovery: The Aftermath of Violence—From Domestic Abuse to Political Terror.* New York: Basic Books, 1997.

Chapter 4

1. See Lerner, Harriet. *The Dance of Connection*. New York: William Morrow Paperbacks, 2002.

2. See Schwartz, Richard C. *Introduction to the Internal Family Systems Model*. Oak Park, IL: Trailheads Publications, 2001.

3. Lerner, Harriet. *The Dance of Intimacy*. New York: HarperCollins, 1989.

4. Of course, the sexual objectification of women and girls was not a new phenomenon; it simply became more overt and infused in women's gender identity.

5. As noted in Chapter 3, power over dynamics are the dynamics of addiction and trauma. Interestingly, psychologist Anne Wilson Schaef and organizational consultant Diane Fassel observed that when one or more members of a family suffer from addiction, the whole family system can take on the personality and behaviors of an addicted individual. Schaef and Fassel named such systems "addictive systems," describing them as closed systems that are organized around maintaining the defensive mentality and behaviors of addiction. More recent examinations of family systems have shown that it's actually not necessary for an addicted individual to be present for the dynamics of an addictive system to exist; similar dynamics have been found in families where trauma and other forms of relational dysfunction have been present. It's important to note that family systems in which addiction or trauma are present don't necessarily become nonrelational, and when they do become nonrelational, this is not an indicator that the members don't care about one another or are not trying to resolve the problem. In many nonrelational family systems, members are simply coping with difficulties the best way they know how. See Schaef, Anne Wilson, and Diane Fassel. *The Addictive Organization: Why We Overwork, Cover Up, Pick Up the Pieces, Please the Boss, and Perpetuate Sick Organizations*. San Francisco: HarperOne, 1990; Schaef, Anne Wilson. *When Society Becomes an Addict*. San Francisco: HarperSanFrancisco, 1987.

6. Allan G. Johnson describes what he calls "systems of privilege" in his excellent text *Privilege, Power, and Difference*. Nonrelational social

systems are similar to systems of privilege, but with dimensions that extend beyond what Johnson describes in his work. Johnson, Allan G. *Privilege, Power, and Difference*. New York: McGraw-Hill Education, 2005.

7.   See Eisler, Riane. *The Chalice and the Blade: Our History, Our Future*. San Francisco: HarperOne, 2011.

8.   Patricia Hill Collins suggests that there is a "matrix of domination" in which people who are oppressed are placed in categories based on such criteria as race, class, and sexual orientation, and then judged as deviant and inferior when measured against the qualities and values of the dominant group. Collins, Patricia Hill. *Black Feminist Thought: Knowledge, Consciousness, and the Politics of Empowerment*. Boston: Unwin Hyman, 1990.

9.   Feminist theologian Elisabeth Schüssler Fiorenza proposed the concept of *kyriarchy*, a system of domination that is similar to patriarchy but that extends beyond gender. Kyriarchy, however, does not account for human–nonhuman relations (relations that include nonhuman animals and the environment), nor is it based on a psychological framework, so I have not used it as the basis of my work here.

10. The notion of interlocking oppressions emerged in large part from the work of Kimberlé Crenshaw, who introduced the concept of intersectionality. See Crenshaw, Kimberlé. "Demarginalizing the Intersection of Race and Sex: A Black Feminist Critique of Antidiscrimination Doctrine, Feminist Theory and Antiracist Politics." *University of Chicago Legal Forum*, no. 1 (1989): art. 8. http:// chicagounbound.uchicago.edu/uclf/vol1989/iss1/8.

11. For an inspiring and insightful read on aging, see *Doing 60 & 70* by Gloria Steinem.

12. See Butler, Robert, N. "Successful Aging and the Role of the Life Review." *Journal of the American Geriatrics Society* 22 (1974): 529–35. doi:10.1111/j.1532-5415.1974.tb04823.x. See also Applewhite, Ashton. *This Chair Rocks: A Manifesto against Ageism*. New York: Macmillan, 2019; and Lamb, Sarah, ed. *Successful Aging as a Contemporary Obsession*. New Brunswick, NJ: Rutgers University Press, 2017.

13. Robbins-Ruszkowski, Jessica. "Aspiring to Activity: Universities of the Third Age, Gardening, and Other Forms of Living in Postsocialist Poland." In *Successful Aging*, edited by Lamb, 112–25.

14. See Lamb, *Successful Aging.*

15. I am describing binary groups to demonstrate how these groups are typically framed in a nonrelational system, and I acknowledge that binaries are often social constructs.

16. The terms *majority* and *minority* were once used to describe members of dominant and nondominant groups, but these terms have been misconstrued. Although they refer to groups that hold the majority or minority of power, most people interpret these terms as referring to groups that make up more or less of the population.

17. McConnell, Allen, and Jill Leibold. "Relations among the Implicit Association Test, Discriminatory Behavior, and Explicit Measures of Racial Attitudes." *Journal of Experimental Social Psychology* 37 (2001): 435–42. https://doi.org/10.1006/jesp.2000.1470; Mahzarin, Banaji, and Jerry Kang. "Fair Measures: A Behavioral Realist Revision of Affirmative Action." *California Law Review* 94 (2006). https://doi.org/10.15779/Z38370Q; Greenwald, Anthony, and Linda Krieger. "Implicit Bias: Scientific Foundations." *California Law Review* 94, no. 4 (2006): 945–68. https://doi.org/10.15779/Z38GH7F.

18. She, Hsiao-Ching. "The Interplay of a Biology Teacher's Beliefs, Teaching Practices and Gender-Based Student-Teacher Classroom Interaction." *Educational Research* 42, no. 1 (2000): 100–11, doi:10.1080/001318800363953; McClowry, Sandra. "Teacher/Student Interactions and Classroom Behavior: The Role of Student Temperament and Gender." *Journal of Research in Childhood Education* 27, no. 3 (2013). doi:10.1080/02568543.2013.796330.

19. Johnson, *Privilege.*

20. Even when powerholders are conscious of the controlling tactics they use in relationships, the non-powerholders are usually not aware of the roles and rules that maintain nonrelationality.

21. These myths share some commonalities with, but are distinct from, the legitimizing myths that justify social dominance, as put forth by Jim Sidanius. See Sidanius, Jim, Erik Devereux, and Felicia Pratto.

"A Comparison of Symbolic Racism Theory and Social Dominance Theory as Explanations for Racial Policy Attitude." *Journal of Social Psychology* 132, no. 3 (1992): 377–95.

22. Cognitive distortions are commonly referred to as "psychological defense mechanisms," and I use this more common phrase in my other writings. However, in this book, I use the term *cognitive distortions* to avoid confusing readers by using "defense" to describe one of three defenses.

Chapter 5

1. This paragraph was first published in Joy, Melanie. *Beyond Beliefs: A Guide to Improving Relationships and Communication for Vegans, Vegetarians, and Meat-Eaters.* New York: Lantern Books, 2018.

2. Kowol, Adam. "The Theory of Cognitive Dissonance." Personal website of Adam Kowol, 2008. http://adamkowol.info/works/Festinger.pdf; Breslavs, Gershon M. "Moral Emotions, Conscience, and Cognitive Dissonance." *Psychology of Thinking* 6, no. 4 (2013): 65–72.

3. See Festinger, Leon. *A Theory of Cognitive Dissonance.* Stanford, CA: Stanford University Press, 1957.

4. For more information on carnism, see Joy, Melanie. *Why We Love Dogs, Eat Pigs, and Wear Cows: An Introduction to Carnism.* 10th anniversary edition. Newburyport, MA: Red Wheel/Weiser, 2020; and Joy, Melanie. "Beyond Carnism and Toward Rational, Authentic Food Choices." TEDx. February 5, 2015. https://www.youtube.com/watch?v=o0VrZPBskpg. Available at https://www.carnism.org.

5. Many of the defenses in this chapter apply to interpersonal nonrelationality as well.

6. I acknowledge that there are many individuals who are not in a position to make their food choices freely, such as those who are economically disadvantaged or geographically unable to access a variety of foods.

7. See Hedges, Chris. *What Every Person Should Know about War.* New York: Free Press, 2003; and "FAOSTAT: Livestock Primary." Food and Agriculture Organization of the United Nations, 2017, https://

data.apps.fao.org/catalog/dataset/livestock-primary-national-global-annual.

8. The small percentage of farmed animals who are "humanely" raised also suffer intensely. Many of these individuals are raised in similar circumstances to those in factory farms, and virtually all of them are ultimately sent to the same slaughterhouses that are used for factory-farmed animals.

9. Dawkins, Marian. "The Science of Animal Suffering." *Ethology* 114, no. 10 (2008): 937–45. doi:10.1111/j.1439-0310.2008.01557.x.

10. BBC News. "Breonna Taylor: Ex-officer Pleads Guilty to Helping Falsify Search Warrant." August 23, 2022. https://www.bbc.co.uk/news/world-us-canada-62635272.

11. "Police Killings of Blacks: Do Black Lives Matter?" Data from 2015-2019. *Society Pages*, 2020. https://thesocietypages.org/toolbox/police-killing-of-blacks/.

12. For an overview of the politics of police killings of BIPOC in the United States, see Martinot, Steve. "On the Epidemic of Police Killings." *Social Justice* 39, no. 4 (2014): 52–75.

13. A cisgender individual has a gender identity (e.g., man or woman) that corresponds to their assigned sex at birth. A gender-conforming individual behaves in ways that conform with gender expectations, for example, wearing pants rather than a skirt if they're a man or shaving their legs if they're a woman.

14. Although the stoning of women is no longer practiced in much of the world, in some places, it is still acceptable.

15. In some societies and languages, it is still normal to use the term *invalid*.

16. Although some societies have made significant improvements to be more accessible to individuals who have disabilities, there is still much progress to be made to truly meet their needs and respect their rights.

17. See Fine, Cordelia. "The Most Neurosexist Study of the Year?" *Slate*, December 4, 2013. http://www.slate.com/articles/health_and_science/science/2013/12/hard_wired_brain_differences_critique_of_male_female_neuroscience_imaging.html; and Fine, Cordelia. *Delusions of Gender: How Our Minds, Society, and Neurosexism*

Create Difference. New York: Norton, 2010. See also the work of Dr. Anne Fausto-Sterling under "Articles" on her website: http://www.annefaustosterling.com/articles/.

18. *Broadcasting Genocide: Censorship, Propaganda & State-Sponsored Violence in Rwanda 1990–1994*. Article 19, p. 67. https://www.article19.org/data/files/pdfs/publications/rwanda-broadcasting-genocide.pdf.

19. "Goebbels Claims Jews Will Destroy Culture." Video. *Holocaust Encyclopedia*. United States Holocaust Memorial Museum. https://encyclopedia.ushmm.org/content/en/film/goebbels-claims-jews-will-destroy-culture.

20. Disability rights activist Stella Young coined the phrase *inspiration porn* to describe media that sensationalizes people with disabilities, depicting them as inspirational solely or partly due to their disabilities. Grue, Jan. "The Problem with Inspiration Porn: A Tentative Definition and a Provisional Critique." *Disability & Society* 31, no. 6 (2016): 838–49. doi:10.1080/09687599.2016.1205473.

21. Often, the proponents of a countersystem are members of the nondominant group most impacted by the nonrelational social system being challenged—for instance, many antiracism advocates are BIPOC. Other times, as is the case with vegans, the proponents are not directly oppressed by the nonrelational system but are advocates for the victims. It's important to note, however, that even when advocates are not direct victims, they may still constitute a nondominant (and sometimes marginalized) group within the system. Vegans, for example, are ideological minorities. Although their minority status and experience are obviously quite different from those of Muslims or women, for instance, they do face certain forms of prejudice and discrimination, and when interacting with nonvegans (all other social power roles being equal), they are often on the lower end of an invisible power differential.

22. Hancock, Adrienne B., and Benjamin A. Rubin. "Influence of Communication Partner's Gender on Language." *Journal of Language and Society* 34, no. 1 (2015): 46–64.

23. James, Deborah, and Sandra Clarke. "Women, Men, and Interruptions." In *Gender and Conversational Interaction*, edited by Deborah Tannen. Oxford Studies in Sociolinguistics. Oxford: Oxford University Press, 1993, pp. 231–80.

24. See, for example, Vernasco, Lucy. "Seven Studies Proving Mansplaining Exists." *Bitchmedia*, July 14, 2014. https://www.bitchmedia.org/post/seven-studies-proving-mansplaining-exists.

25. "Understanding and Addressing Violence against Women: Intimate Partner Violence." World Health Organization and Pan American Health Organization, 2012. http://www.who.int/int/iris/handle/10665/77432.

26. In 2010, an average of twenty people every minute experienced intimate partner physical violence in the United States alone—amounting to more than ten million abuse victims per year. Black, Michele C., Kathleen C. Basile, Matthew J. Breiding, Sharon G. Smith, Mikel L. Walters, Melissa T. Merrick, Jieru Chen, and Mark R. Stevens. *National Intimate Partner and Sexual Violence Survey: 2010 Summary Report*. Atlanta, GA: National Center for Injury Prevention and Control, Centers for Disease Control and Prevention, 2010. http://www.cdc.gov/violenceprevention/pdf/nisvs_report2010-a.pdf.

27. Bancroft, Lundy. *Why Does He Do That? Inside the Minds of Angry and Controlling Men.* New York: Berkeley Books, 2002. See also Harris, Tal, Laurie B. Moret, Jerry Gale, and Karen L. Kampmeyer. "Therapists' Gender Assumptions and How These Assumptions Influence Therapy." *Journal of Feminist Family Therapy* 12, nos. 2–3 (2001): 33–59. doi:10.1300/J086v12n02_02.

28. Although one's projections onto another (or others) sometimes involve unconscious impulses or qualities, this section is not referring to projection in that strict Freudian sense of the term.

29. Lamb-Books, Benjamin. *Angry Abolitionists and the Rhetoric of Slavery—Moral Emotions in Social Movements.* London: Palgrave Macmillan, 2016.

30. See "This Is How Misogynists Tried to Stop Women from Winning the Vote." Stylist Magazine; Susan Devaney. Retrieved March 20, 2023.

https://www.stylist.co.uk/visible-women/misogynists-anti-suffragette-illustrations-stop-women-win-vote-history-features/187998.

31. See, for example, "White Riots Versus Black Protests." Everyday Feminism and Brave New Films. Retrieved March 20, 2023.https://everydayfeminism.com/2015/12/white-riots-vs-black-protests/.

32. In "Working through Environmental Despair," Joanna Macy writes: "People are inhibited from expressing their anxieties because they feel that in order to do so they need to be walking data banks and skillful debaters. Taking action on behalf of our common world has unfortunately become confused with winning an argument." Macy, Joanna. "Working through Environmental Despair." In *Ecopsychology: Restoring the Earth, Healing the Mind*, edited by Theodore Roszak, Mary E. Gomes, and Allen D. Kanner, 240–62. San Francisco: Sierra Club Books, 1995.

33. See Fiske, Susan T., Amy J.C. Cuddy, and Peter Glick. "Universal Dimensions of Social Cognition: Warmth and Competence." *Trends in Cognitive Sciences* 11, no. 2 (February 2007): 77–83.

34. Cartwright, Samuel. "Diseases and Peculiarities of the Negro Race." *DeBrow's Review*, AMS Press, 1851.

35. Drescher, Jack. "Out of DSM: Depathologizing Homosexuality." *Behavioral Sciences* 5, no. 4 (December 4, 2015): 565–75. https://www.ncbi.nlm.nih.gov/pmc/articles/PMC4695779/. doi:10.3390/bs5040565.

36. See Woodward, Colin Edward. *Marching Masters: Slavery, Race, and the Confederate Army during the Civil War*. Charlottesville: University of Virginia Press, 2014. https://muse.jhu.edu/book/28770.

37. Bargh, John. "The Cognitive Monster: The Case against the Controllability of Automatic Stereotype Effects." In *Dual-Process Theories in Social Psychology*, edited by Shelley Chaiken, 361–82. New York: Guilford Press, 1999; Gerostathos, Antonios, Yvesde Roten, Sylvie Berney, Jean-Nicolas Despland, and Gilles Ambresin. "How Does Addressing Patient's Defenses Help to Repair Alliance Ruptures in Psychodynamic Psychotherapy?" *Journal of Nervous and Mental Disease* 202, no. 5 (2014): 419–24. doi:10.1097/NMD.0000000000000112.

38. *Livestock's Long Shadow: Environmental Issues and Options.* Livestock, Environment, and Development Initiative, 2006. http://www.fao.org/docrep/010/a0701e/a0701e.pdf.

Chapter 6

1. "Cassies 2008 Cases: Case Name: New Diamond Shreddies." https://www.studocu.com/en-ca/document/brock-university/marketing-basics/shreddies-imc-campaign-2008-copy/10643732.

2. Our inborn traits, such as our aptitude for introversion or extraversion, also play a role in determining the narratives we construct.

3. See Bush, Julia. "The Anti-Suffrage Movement." *Votes for Women.* British Library, March 5, 2018. https://www.bl.uk/votes-for-women/articles/the-anti-suffrage-movement. See also Jorgensen-Earp, Cheryl R., and Darwin D. Jorgensen. "Physiology and Physical Force: The Effect of Edwardian Science on Women's Suffrage." *Southern Communication Journal* 81, no. 3 (2016): 136–55. doi:10.1080/104 1794X.2015.1124914.

4. Early scholarship on dominant narratives was published by American sociologist W.E.B. Du Bois in *The Souls of Black Folk* (Chicago: A.C. McClurg & Co., 1903). His references to "the color line," "the veil," and "double-consciousness" describe the operation of a dominant white narrative without using the term explicitly. Developments in sociology and critical theory later in the century saw the conceptual emergence of metanarratives (Jean-Francois Lyotard. *The Postmodern Condition.* Translated by Geoff Bennington and Brian Massumi. Minneapolis: University of Minnesota Press, 1984) and discourses (Michel Foucault. *The Archaeology of Knowledge.* Translated by Alan Sheridan. New York: Pantheon Books, 1972), which arguably laid the theoretical groundwork for the eventual emergence of "dominant narratives." Kimberlé Crenshaw's work on intersectionality uses the phrases "dominant ways of thinking," "dominant view," "dominant group control," and "dominant norm," laying further foundations for the current ubiquity of the phrase "dominant (white) narrative." See Crenshaw, Kimberlé. "Demarginalizing the Intersection of Race and Sex: A Black Feminist Critique of Antidiscrimination Doctrine,

Feminist Theory and Antiracist Politics." *University of Chicago Legal Forum*, no. 1 (1989): art. 8. http://chicagounbound.uchicago.edu/uclf/vol1989/iss1/8.

5. Zhao, Yue, Richard Montoro, Karine Igartua, and Brett D. Thombs. "Suicidal Ideation and Attempt among Adolescents Reporting 'Unsure' Sexual Identity or Heterosexual Identity Plus Same-Sex Attraction or Behavior: Forgotten Groups." *Journal of the American Academy of Child and Adolescent Psychiatry* 49, no. 2 (2010): 104–13.

6. Haidt, Jonathan. *The Righteous Mind: Why Good People Are Divided by Politics and Religion.* New York: Pantheon Books, 2012.

7. See Applewhite, Ashton. *This Chair Rocks: A Manifesto against Ageism.* New York: Macmillan, 2019.

8. This idea is similar to that of false consciousness as described by Marxist philosophers; see, for example, Lukács, György. *History and Class Consciousness: Studies in Marxist Dialectics.* Translated by Roger Livingstone. Cambridge: MIT Press, 1971. Originally published in 1923.

9. After the election of American president Barack Obama, the *Wall Street Journal* published an editorial claiming that "[the nation could] put to rest the myth of racism as a barrier to achievement in this splendid country." "President-Elect Obama." *Wall Street Journal*, November 5, 2008, A22. https://www.wsj.com/articles/SB122586244657800863. See Kendi, Ibram X. "The Heartbeat of Racism Is Denial." *New York Times,* January 13, 2018. https://www.nytimes.com/2018/01/13/opinion/sunday/heartbeat-of-racism-denial.html. See also Eddo-Lodge, Reni. *Why I'm No Longer Talking to White People about Race.* London: Bloomsbury, 2018.

10. Sharman, Jon. "'What You're Seeing Isn't Happening,' Trump Tells Veterans' Convention in Meandering Rant against 'Fake News.'" *Independent*, July 25, 2018. https://www.independent.co.uk/news/world/americas/us-politics/trump-fake-news-veterans-foreign-wars-video-watch-not-happening-a8462711.html.

11. "The Knight/Gallup survey reported that more than 60 percent of the respondents see 'too much bias in the reporting of news stories that are supposed to be objective,' while less than half (44

percent) can identify any news source that they believe reports the news objectively." Knight Foundation. "Why Has Trust in the Government and Media Declined?" *Crisis in Democracy: Renewing Trust in America.* Washington, DC: The Aspen Institute, 2019. See https://kf-site-production.s3.amazonaws.com/media_elements/files/000/000/283/original/Knight_Commission_Report_on_Trust_Media_and_Democracy_FINAL.pdf.

12. Nickerson, Raymond. "Confirmation Bias: A Ubiquitous Phenomenon in Many Guises." *Tufts University Review of General Psychology* 2, no. 2 (1998): 175–220.

13. See Coppola, Al. *The Theatre of Experiment: Staging Natural Philosophy in Eighteenth-Century Britain.* Oxford: Oxford University Press, 2016.

14. W.E.B. Du Bois (*The Souls of Black Folk*) and Franz Fanon (*The Wretched of the Earth.* New York: Grove Press, 1963) were the first to write about the deficiency narrative as it applied to the depiction of Black people living under white supremacy.

15. With an awareness of the limitations of current language, I have done my best to use respectful terminology. I use the term *disability* only when necessary and, whenever appropriate, with person-centered language [saying "a person who has a disability" rather than "a disabled person"].

16. Studies have shown that when we are in positions of power, we are more likely to hold others to higher standards than those to which we hold ourselves—we feel justified breaking rules that we expect others to respect. In other words, we feel that we, unlike others, are entitled to what we want. And the opposite is also true: when we are in non-powerholding positions, we tend to hold ourselves to higher standards than those to which we hold others, and we feel less entitled to break rules and take what we want. See, for example, Robertson, Ian H. "How Power Affects the Brain." *Psychologist* 26 (March 2013): 186–89. https://www.researchgate.net/publication/286534974_How_power_affects_the_brain.

17. "The World's Women 2015. Work. Chapter 4." United Nations—UN Statistics Division, 2015. https://unstats.un.org/unsd/

gender/chapter4/chapter4.html; McHugh, Maureen, and Jennifer Hambaugh. "She Said, He Said: Gender, Language, and Power." *Handbook of Gender Research in Psychology* 1 (2010): 379–410.

18.　Merkel, Wolfgang. "Is Capitalism Compatible with Democracy?" *Comparative Governance and Politics* 8, no. 2 (2014): 109–28; Kornai, Janos. "Centralization and the Capitalist Market Economy." *CESifo Forum* 13, no. 1 (2012): 47–59.

19.　See, for example, Keltner, Dacher. *The Power Paradox: How We Gain and Lose Power.* New York: Penguin, 2016. See also Wang, Meifang, and Feng Yang. "The Malleability of Stereotype Effects on Spontaneous Trait Inferences: The Moderating Role of Perceivers' Power." *Social Psychology* 48 (2017): 3–18. https://doi.org/10.1027/1864-9335/a000288.

20.　Jean Baker Miller points out in *Toward a New Psychology of Women* that to complain is to publicly admit harm, which disrupts the status quo, and that the dominant group tends to suppress complaint through shaming (consider how "complaining" is often feminized and "complainers" are infantilized as "whiners"). Baker Miller, Jean. *Toward a New Psychology of Women.* Boston: Beacon Press, 1987. First published 1976.

21.　"Anti-Semitic Incidents Increasing, ADL Says." National Public Radio, October 28, 2018. https://www.npr.org/2018/10/28/661520291/anti-semitic-incidents-increasing-adl-says.

22.　Patricia Hill Collins proposed the concept of "controlling images," which are false images—such as that of the "savage" Indigenous American—created by the dominant group about members of the nondominant group that prevent the latter from realizing or resisting their oppression. See Collins, Patricia Hill. *Black Feminist Thought: Knowledge, Consciousness, and the Politics of Empowerment.* Boston: Unwin Hyman, 1990.

Chapter 7

1.　Crenshaw, Kimberlé. "The Urgency of Intersectionality." TEDWomen, October 2016. https://www.ted.com/talks/kimberle_crenshaw_the_urgency_of_intersectionality.

2. *Intersectionality* is often used inaccurately to describe the ways that oppressions overlap with and reinforce one another. The actual meaning of the term, which Crenshaw intended to be used as a legal definition, is that oppressions which intersect create a new, distinct category of oppression within which an individual may face a distinct form of discrimination. For example, a Black or Brown woman does not merely face "double" oppression but faces a different type of oppression that leads to a different kind of discrimination compared to a white woman or a Black or Brown man.

3. The concept of privilege is believed to have been first published in 1903 by W.E.B. Du Bois in his essay *The Souls of Black Folk*; it was later popularized through Peggy McIntosh's 1988 essay "White Privilege and Male Privilege: A Personal Account of Coming to See Correspondences through Work in Women's Studies." (Working paper 189. Wellesley, MA: Center for Research on Women, 1988. Available online at https://www.wcwonline.org/Fact-Sheets-Briefs/white-privilege-and-male-privilege-a-personal-account-of-coming-to-see-correspondences-through-work-in-women-s-studies-2).

4. Sherer, Mark, James E. Maddux, Blaise Mercandante, Steven Prentice-Dunn, Beth Jacobs, and Ronald W. Rogers. "The Self-Efficacy Scale: Construction and Validation." *Psychological Reports* 51, no. 2 (1982): 663–71.

5. McNamee, Stephen J., and Robert B. Miller Jr. *The Meritocracy Myth.* Lanham, MD: Rowman & Littlefield, 2004.

6. Nagahawatte, Tanya N., and Robert L. Goldenberg. "Poverty, Maternal Health, and Adverse Pregnancy Outcomes." *Annals of the New York Academy of Sciences* 1136 (2008): 80–85.

7. Clark, Kenneth B., and Mamie P. Clark. "Emotional Factors in Racial Identification and Preference in Negro Children." *The Journal of Negro Education* 19, no. 3 (Summer, 1950): 341–50. http://www.jstor.org/stable/2966491; Jordan, Phillip, and Maria Hernandez-Reif. "Reexamination of Young Children's Racial Attitudes and Skin Tone Preferences." *Journal of Black Psychology* 35, no. 3 (2009): 388–403.

8. If, however, the person crossing our boundary has more social power than we do and especially if we perceive that power as deserved— if they are someone famous, for example—we may be less likely to notice or be offended by the violation.

9. Johnson, Allan G. *Privilege, Power, and Difference.* New York: McGraw-Hill Education, 2005.

10. Ferguson, Sian. "Privilege 101: A Quick and Dirty Guide," September 29, 2014, p. 5. https://theavarnagroup.com/wp-content/uploads/2016/01/Privilege-101.pdf.

11. See, for example, DiAngelo, Robin. *White Fragility: Why It's So Hard for White People to Talk about Racism.* Boston: Beacon Press, 2018.

12. For an excellent resource for understanding and navigating privilege, as well as building resilience, see Chugh, Dolly. *A More Just Future.* New York: Atria Books, 2022.

13. Hänsel, Alexander, and Roland von Känel. "The Ventro-Medial Prefrontal Cortex: A Major Link between the Autonomic Nervous System, Regulation of Emotion, and Stress Reactivity?" *BioPsychoSocial Medicine* 2, no. 21 (2008). doi:10.1186/1751-0759-2-21. See also Mobbs, Dean, Predrag Petrovic, Jennifer L. Marchant, Demis Hassabis, Nikolaus Weiskopf, Ben Seymour, Raymond J. Dolan, and Christopher D. Frith. "When Fear Is Near: Threat Imminence Elicits Prefrontal-Periaqueductal Gray Shifts in Humans." *Science*, August 24, 2007, 1079–83.

14. Dr. A. Breeze Harper's experiences as a vegan activist are telling: "I have faced opposition really only from post-racial white middle class vegans who are 'single issue' and are so invested in their racial-class privilege (at the unconscious level in many cases) that they simply cannot admit that white privilege, race and class still matter in the USA." See Petersson-Martin, Kira. "#TBT: An interview with Dr. A. Breeze Harper." *T.O.F.U. Magazine*, May 2016. ilovetofu.ca/2016/05/05/tbt-an-interview-with-dr-a-breeze-harper/.

15. See Larson, Stephanie Greco. *Media and Minorities: The Politics of Race in News and Entertainment.* New York: Rowman & Littlefield, 2006.

16. Duarte, José L., Jarret T. Crawford, Charlotta Stern, Jonathan Haidt, Lee J. Philip, and Philip E. Tetlock. "Political Diversity Will Improve

Social Psychological Science." *Behavioural and Brain Sciences* 38 (2015), E130. doi:10.1017/S0140525X1400043.

17. Of course, it's also important for us to be literate around privilege when we're a member of a group that's been oppressed, but a just redistribution of power requires that more of the burden of transformation be carried by those who have benefited from a nonrelational system.

18. Emotional labor is the uncompensated work of managing essential yet often invisible tasks involving emotion.

Chapter 8

1. Linda Hartling and Elizabeth Sparks describe systems other than power over systems as "cultures of connection," suggesting they are organized around "growth through relationship, mutual empowerment, responsiveness, authenticity, and movement toward mutuality." Hartling, Linda, and Elizabeth Sparks. "Relational Cultural Practice: Working in a Nonrelational World." In *The Power of Connection: Recent Developments in Relational-Cultural Theory*, edited by Judith V. Jordan, 162. New York: Routledge, 2010.

2. It is interesting to note that of the five moral values that inform one's political orientation, compassion and justice—the two values that underlie progressive politics—may be the most likely to balance power. The other three values are loyalty/in-group standing, authority/respect, and purity/sanctity. For more information on moral values and political orientations, see MoralFoundations.org and YourMorals.org.

3. Although feminism emerged as a countersystem to the nonrelational system of patriarchy, it has not been without problems. As with all systems, including countersystems, feminism must continue to examine its own assumptions and grow in integrity. For example, traditional feminism has rightly been criticized for being a movement of and for white women.

4. Nhat Hanh, Thich. *Interbeing.* New Delhi: Full Circle, 2009.

5. "I have a dream that one day this nation will rise up and live out the true meaning of its creed: 'We hold these truths to be self-evident, that all men are created equal.'" King, Martin L., Jr. "I Have a Dream."

Speech at the Lincoln Memorial, Washington, DC, August 28, 1963. Available at American Rhetoric. https://www.americanrhetoric.com/speeches/mlkihaveadream.htm.

6. These are not to be confused with Hartling and Sparks's "pseudorelational cultures," which are systems with conflict-averse participants who avoid authenticity in order to keep the peace. Hartling and Sparks, "Relational Cultural Practice." In *Power of Connection*, edited by Jordan, 158–81.

7. Note that here I am referring to all types of fundamentalist systems, not only religious ones.

8. For an excellent book on preventing and treating this kind of traumatic stress, see van Dernoot Lipsky, Laura, and Connie Burk. *Trauma Stewardship*. Oakland, CA: Berrett-Koehler, 2009.

9. Coddington, Kate. "Contagious Trauma: Reframing the Spatial Mobility of Trauma within Advocacy Work." *Emotion, Space and Society* 24 (August 2017): 66–73.

10. For an informative discussion on resilience and relationality, see Hartling, Linda M. "Strengthening Resilience in a Risky World: It's All about Relationships." In *Power of Connection*, edited by Jordan, 49–68.

11. As mentioned in Chapter 6, examining the potential impact of traumatization on advocates of countersystems is not meant to pathologize them or discredit their actions. It is simply meant to point out that power over dynamics can and often do end up being recreated when there is a lack of awareness of the process of power, and particularly when certain aggravating factors, such as traumatization, are present.

12. Wilkins, Clara L., and Cheryl R. Kaiser. "Racial Progress as Threat to the Status Hierarchy: Implications for Perceptions of Anti-White Bias." *Psychological Science* 25, no. 2 (February 2014): 439–46. doi:10.1177/0956797613508412.

13. The rise since the 1970s of the men's rights movement, which was sparked as a "counterrevolution" to the second wave of feminism, is a clear example of this. Notable groups include Men's Rights Incorporated, the National Coalition for Men, and the National Organization of Men.

14. Hicks, Donna. *Dignity: The Essential Role It Plays in Resolving Conflict*. New Haven, CT: Yale University Press, 2011.

15. Hicks, *Dignity*.

16. Goleman, Daniel. *Emotional Intelligence: Why It Can Matter More than IQ*. New York: Bantam, 1995.

17. See Lakin, Jessica L., Valerie E. Jefferis, Clara Michelle Cheng, and Tanya L. Chartrand. "The Chameleon Effect as Social Glue: Evidence for the Evolutionary Significance of Nonconscious Mimicry." *Journal of Nonverbal Behavior* 27 (2003): 145–62. doi:10.1023/A:1025389814290. See also Chartrand, Tanya L., and John A. Bargh. "The Chameleon Effect: The Perception-Behavior Link and Social Interaction." *Journal of Personality and Social Psychology* 76 (1999): 893–910.

18. Zenger, Jack, and Joseph Folkman. "The Ideal Praise-to-Criticism Ratio." *Harvard Business Review*, March 15, 2013. https://hbr.org/2013/03/the-ideal-praise-to-criticism.

19. Tugend, Alina. "Praise Is Fleeting, but Brickbats We Recall." *New York Times*, March 23, 2012. https://www.nytimes.com/2012/03/24/your-money/why-people-remember-negative-events-more-than-positive-ones.html.

20. Foulk, Trevor, Andrew Woolum, and Amir Erez. "Catching Rudeness Is Like Catching a Cold: The Contagion Effects of Low-Intensity Negative Behaviors." *Journal of Applied Psychology* 101, no. 1 (June 29, 2015): 50–67. doi:10.1037/apl0000037.

21. This notion is similar to Eckhart Tolle's description of the ego. See Tolle, Eckhart. *The Power of Now: A Guide to Spiritual Enlightenment*. Novato, CA: New World Library, 1999.

22. See "Trauma as a Precursor to Violent Extremism." START, April 2015. https://www.start.umd.edu/pubs/START_CSTAB_TraumaAsPrecursortoViolentExtremism_April2015.pdf.

23. See Picciolini, Christian. *Romantic Violence: Memoirs of an American Skinhead*. Chicago: Goldmill Group, 2015.

24. See, for example, Keltner, Dacher. *The Power Paradox: How We Gain and Lose Power*. New York: Penguin, 2016.

25. For more information on how having power affects perceptions

and behaviors, see Keltner, *The Power Paradox*; Guinote, Ana, and Theresa K. Vescio (eds.). *The Social Psychology of Power*. New York: Guildford Press, 2010.

26. Brown, Brené. *Dare to Lead*. New York: Penguin Random House, 2018.

27. There is evidence of a natural progression from competitive toward cooperative game-playing strategies when the latter are sufficiently rewarded, and the rewarding is itself a form of cooperation. See Tampuu, Ardi, Tambet Matiisen, Dorian Kodelja, Ilya Kuzovkin, Kristjan Korjus, Juhan Aru, Jaan Aru, and Raul Vicente. "Multiagent Cooperation and Competition with Deep Reinforcement Learning." *PLoS ONE* 12, no. 4 (April 5, 2017): e0172395. doi:10.1371/journal.pone.0172395.

28. Lerner, Harriet. *The Dance of Connection*. New York: William Morrow Paperbacks, 2002.

Chapter 9

1. Tod, David, James Hardy, and Emily Oliver. "Effects of Self-Talk: A Systematic Review." *Journal of Sport & Exercise Psychology* 33 (2011): 666–87. doi:10.1123/jsep.33.5.666.

2. See McKay, Matthew, Martha Davis, and Patrick Fanning. *Messages: The Communication Skills Book*. Oakland, CA: New Harbinger, 2009.

3. Nonviolent communication was developed by Marshall Rosenberg (see Rosenberg, Marshall B. *Nonviolent Communication: A Language of Life*. Encinitas, CA: PuddleDancer Press, 2015). I recommend a slightly modified version of the original method, as put forth in *Messages* by McKay, Davis, and Fanning.

4. Rosenberg, *Nonviolent Communication*.

5. Fletcher, Clive, and Caroline Bailey. "Assessing Self-Awareness: Some Issues and Methods." *Journal of Managerial Psychology* 18, no. 5 (2003): 395–404. doi:10.1108/02683940310484008.

6. Two excellent resources for learning to self-regulate and help others regulate are Campbell, Susan. *From Triggered to Tranquil: How Self-Compassion and Mindful Presence Can Transform Relationship Conflicts and Heal Childhood Wounds*. Novato, CA: New World

Library, 2021; and Haines, Staci. *The Politics of Trauma: Somatics, Healing, and Social Justice.* Berkeley, CA: North Atlantic Books, 2019. *The Politics of Trauma* is also a powerful guide to building resilient movements for social change.

7. Vago, David R., and David A. Silbersweig. "Self-Awareness, Self-Regulation, and Self-Transcendence (S-ART): A Framework for Understanding the Neurobiological Mechanisms of Mindfulness." *Frontiers of Human Neuroscience*, October 25, 2012. www.ncbi.nlm.nih.gov/pubmed/23112770.

8. Tang, Yi-Yuan, Qilin Lu, Xiujuan Geng, Elliot A. Stein, Yihong Yang, and Michael I. Posner. "Short-Term Meditation Induces White Matter Changes in the Anterior Cingulate." *PNAS* 107, no. 35 (August 31, 2010): 15649–52. doi:10.1073/pnas.1011043107.

9. Learning cognitive-behavioral therapy (CBT) is an excellent way to develop the inner observer.

10. Mengran Xu, Christine Purdon, Paul Seli, and Daniel Smilek. "Mindfulness and Mind Wandering: The Protective Effects of Brief Meditation in Anxious Individuals." *Consciousness and Cognition* 51 (2017): 157.

Chapter 10

1. For an examination of how people use their roles to support or challenge nonrelational behaviors and systems, see Bazerman, Max. *Complicit: How We Enable the Unethical and How to Stop.* Princeton, NJ: Princeton University Press, 2022.

2. Ko, Aph, and Syl Ko. *Aphro-ism: Essays on Pop Culture, Feminism, and Black Veganism from Two Sisters.* New York: Lantern Books, 2017. Also see Lorde, Audre. "The Great American Disease." *Black Scholar* 10, no. 8/9 (1979): 17–20.

3. For excellent resources on privilege, see David, E.J.R., and Annie O. Derthick. *The Psychology of Oppression.* New York: Springer, 2017; and Johnson, Allan G. *Privilege, Power, and Difference.* New York: McGraw-Hill Education, 2005.

4. "The Facts behind the #metoo Movement: A National Study on Sexual Harassment and Assault." Stop Street Harassment, February 2018.

http://www.stopstreetharassment.org/wp-content/uploads/2018/01/ Full-Report-2018-National-Study-on-Sexual-Harassment-and-Assault. pdf; "Victims of Sexual Violence: Statistics." RAINN, 2018. https:// www.rainn.org/statistics/victims-sexual-violence.

5. Herman, Judith. *Trauma and Recovery: The Aftermath of Violence— From Domestic Abuse to Political Terror.* New York: Basic Books, 2015. First published 1992. See also Courtois, Christine A. "Complex Trauma, Complex Reactions: Assessment and Treatment." *Psychological Trauma: Theory, Research, Practice, and Policy* S, no. 1 (2008): 86–100. doi:10.1037/1942-9681.S.1.86.

6. Weingarten, Kaethe. *Common Shock: Witnessing Violence Every Day—How We Are Harmed, How We Can Heal.* New York: Dutton, 2003.

7. See "Press Releases: Facing the Truth." BBC, September 24, 2014. http://www.bbc.co.uk/pressoffice/pressreleases/stories/2006/02_ february/14/truth.shtml.

8. See works by Terrence Real—for example, *Terry Real: New Rules for Couples* and *Us: Getting Past You and Me to Build a More Loving Relationship.* Relational Life Institute, 2017. http://www.terryreal.com/.

9. In describing the rigidity and porousness of psychological boundaries, my intention is not to oversimplify this complex issue but to point out a key way that boundaries can be affected by privilege and oppression. It is also worth noting that one of the central features of trauma is its impact on psychological boundaries: trauma involves boundary violations, often by once-trusted individuals, and it can cause survivors to struggle to develop secure psychological boundaries. Those who are targets of oppression may have a similar struggle.

10. Here, I am referring to the treatment of those who are being called out—and about whom the person or people calling them out have little information. I am not referring to deeply problematic, oppressive powerholding individuals and institutions, such as Donald Trump and his administration, whose motivations are well documented and well corroborated.

11. The notion of calling out originated in Black social justice circles as an important way to challenge racism by naming oppressive behaviors and policies and holding the offending individuals and institutions accountable. However, the practice of calling out has become mainstreamed, and it is not always used toward its original ends.

12. See, for example, Erskine, Richard G. "Shame and Self-Righteousness: Transactional Analysis Perspectives and Clinical Interventions." *Transactional Analysis Journal* 24, no. 2 (1994): 86–102.

13. See Trần, Ngọc Loan. "Calling IN: A Less Disposable Way of Holding Each Other Accountable." BGD Blog, December 2013. https://www.bgdblog.org/2013/12/calling-less-disposable-way-holding-accountable/.

Chapter 11

1. Bolden-Barrett, Valerie. "Toxic Cultures Have Cost US Businesses $223B in the Past Five Years." *HR Dive*. September 30, 2019. https://www.hrdive.com/news/toxic-cultures-have-cost-us-businesses-223b-in-the-past-five-years/563905/.

2. Rayner, Charlotte, and Keashly, Loraleigh. "Bullying at Work: A Perspective from Britain and North America." In S. Fox and P. E. Spector (eds.) *Counterproductive Work Behavior: Investigations of Actors and Targets*. Washington, DC: American Psychological Association, 2005: 271–96.

3. For an excellent examination of ingrouping, see Klein, Ezra. *Why We're Polarized*. New York: Avid Reader Press, 2020.

4. This section is based on a comprehensive meta-analysis published by William L. White and William R. Miller. White, William L., and Miller, W. "The Use of Confrontation in Addiction Treatment: History, Science and Time for Change." *Counselor* 8, no. 4 (2007): 12–30.

5. Alcoholics Anonymous and some of the models of psychotherapy that preceded it were distinctly nonconfrontational.

6. Grant, Adam. "The Science of Reasoning with Unreasonable People." *New York Times*. January 31, 2021. https://www.nytimes.com/2021/01/31/opinion/change-someones-mind.html.

7. Grant, "The Science of Reasoning with Unreasonable People."

8. Grant, "The Science of Reasoning with Unreasonable People."

9. See, for example, Hari, Johann. *Stolen Focus: Why You Can't Pay Attention*. London: Bloomsbury, 2022.

10. Tutu, Desmond. "Made for Goodness." (Jan. 12, 2012). Available at: https://www.huffpost.com/entry/made-for-goodness_b_1199864.

11. Lieberman, Matthew D. *Hardwired for Connection: Why Our Brains Are Wired to Connect*. New York: Broadway Books, 2014. See also Banks, Amy, and Leigh Ann Hirschman. *Wired to Connect: The Surprising Link between Brain Science and Strong, Healthy Relationships*. New York: TarcherPerigee, 2016.

INDEX

ABOUT THE AUTHOR

**MELANIE JOY, PhD**, is a psychologist specializing in the psychology of oppression and social transformation and in relationships. She is a long-time advocate for justice and was a lecturer at the University of Massachusetts, Boston, for 11 years, where she taught courses on privilege and oppression, feminist psychology, psychological trauma, and animal rights. Her work has helped explain why individuals and institutions engage in behaviors that harm other people, animals, the planet, and themselves—as well as how to change this pattern.

Joy is the award-winning author of seven books, including the bestselling *Why We Love Dogs, Eat Pigs, and Wear Cows* and *Getting Relationships Right*, and she's the eighth recipient of the Ahimsa Award—previously given to the Dalai Lama and Nelson Mandela—for her work on global nonviolence. She is also an internationally recognized speaker and trainer who's presented her work in 50 countries across six continents, and she's the founding president of the charitable organization Beyond Carnism. You can learn more about her work at carnism.org